D1692857

The Berlin task group of district equal opportunities officers

The Berlin Senate Department for Labour, Integration and Women's Issues, Gender Equality Office

advances
adventures
emotions
atmospheres
travails
tribulations
oases

Pearls on the River Spree

Berlin: City of Women

Foreword

Berlin is full of different paths to follow, ways of looking, opportunities to experience and explore the city. We looked at the city from a woman's perspective, searching for traces and picking up even the tiniest clues. Our aim is to invite Berliners and visitors alike to follow our feminist curiosity about the past and present of Berlin's women. This book offers a panorama of the city. At each location it indicates the presence of women, and especially their efforts to achieve creative spaces, equal rights, and emancipation.

We want to tell a story, not simply draw up a list. That's why we chose keywords that open up stories about how Berlin's women have lived, struggled, worked, loved, and suffered. Women's impact on the city is often hidden, or only emerges at second glance; retracing it takes knowledge, passion, and a spirit of inquiry. The struggles of women for political participation, the right to vote, the power to make decisions about their bodies and their lives, for education and careers, are at the heart of the stories we have chosen. They cover a surprisingly wide spectrum.

Our subject is a city—what happens there, and what happened in the past, always has its own particular location. We present those locations, and often they bring to light things we never expected. The locations reveal actions, changes, and hidden traces, showing what has disappeared, what has been lost, the violence, the many layers and facets that make up the city's complex fabric. The photographs reflect women's witty and sidelong views of this town, and they whet our appetite for more.

Gender Equality Office,
The Berlin Senate Department for Labour, Integration and Women's Issues
The Berlin task group of district equal opportunities officers

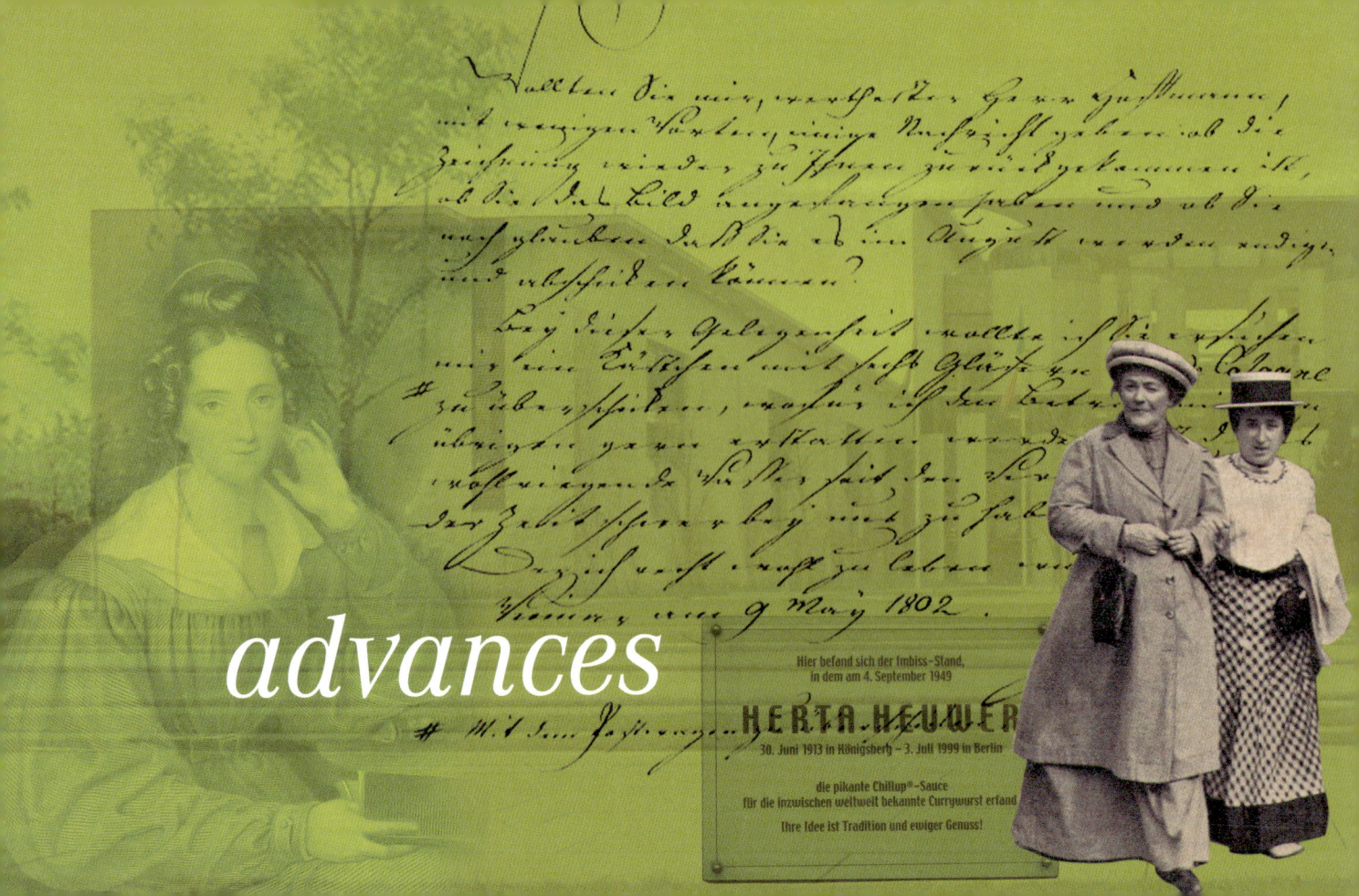

advances

Amazon

advances

From high up on her horse, the gaze of the scantily clothed Amazon roams dispassionately. This strikingly unusual image of female nonchalance was created for the Tiergarten park by Berlin sculptor Louis Tuaillon at the close of the 19th century, years that were not kind to women's politics. Not far from the Reichstag, where a little parliamentarianism was practiced—under Kaiser Wilhelm's control and strictly excluding women—here in the park liberty beckoned, in the beautiful form of a mythological female figure who seems to have set aside not only her clothes but also the chains of a stifling morality and domesticity.

Almost a century after the Amazon was sculpted, small groups of energetic ladies began to be seen gathering at her feet. After drawing inspiration from her, body and soul, they set off together to run through the Tiergarten, causing consternation when they accompanied their gymnastics with yells or jumped boisterously over the legs of sunbathers relaxing on the lawns. Without an arrow or a myth in sight, women were reclaiming the public space, and women's sports and self-defense clubs gave them the weaponry they needed. We don't know what dreams moved the sculptor as he made the Amazon, but for the Berlin women who enjoyed exercise and physical strength long before the days of gyms and women's runs, she was both a meeting point and the focus of their dreams of a freer femininity (➤ **Run, Lola, Run**).

Location
Amazon in the Tiergarten Park
Ben-Gurion-Strasse
10765 Berlin

How to get there
S 1, 2, 25,
U 55 Brandenburger Tor,
Bus 200 Tiergartenstrasse

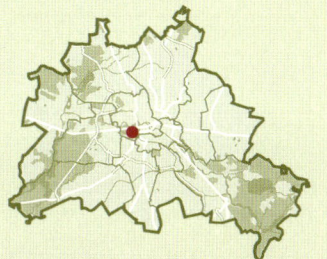

The dream of a freer femininity

Dada

advances

World War I brought the orderly, class-based society of the German Empire crashing down. Harmony, balance, aesthetic beauty—the time for artistic ideals like those had passed. The Dada Club gave radical expression to a noisy rebellion against existing values, education, bourgeoisie, tradition. Dadaism questioned everything. Everything? No, one tradition remained untouched: the patriarchal claim to superiority, expressed in misogyny in general and denigration of women artists in particular (→ Painting ladies). The Dadaists rebelled not *against* patriarchy, but on its foundations. Nevertheless, women artists joined in exploiting the new departures in art. They attacked the traditional framework of aesthetics, morality, and society. Perhaps the most impressive was Hannah Höch (1889–1978), who today enjoys the very un-Dadaistic reputation of being Dadaism's *grande dame*.

Hannah Höch came to Berlin from Gotha as a young woman. She studied art, worked as a draftswoman and in her own studio in the Friedenau district, and managed to earn her living as an artist. Her collages and photomontages gave fiercely critical voice to her era's turmoil and to her experience as a woman and artist. In 1920, she was the only woman involved in the "First International Dada Fair."

Vilified by the Nazis as "degenerate," Höch managed to disappear almost entirely from public view in her little house in Heiligensee. She survived the "Thousand-Year Reich" in seclusion, and created a spectacular garden that supplied her with motifs for her art. Today, Hannah Höch's house and garden are open to the public, as a memorial to a great artist who provided the missing component in the Dadaists' revolution: the dynamite to explode art's patriarchal foundations.

Location
Künstlerhaus Hannah Höch
An der Wildbahn 33
13503 Berlin
Viewing by arrangement
tel. +49 (0) 30 4314824

How to get there
S 25 Schulzendorf (near Tegel)

Sources
www.hannah-hoech-haus-ev.de
www.reinickendorf.de

To find out more

www.hannah-hoech-archiv.de

Julia Dech and Ellen Maurer (eds), *Da-da-zwischen-Reden zu Hannah Höch*, Berlin: Orlanda, 1991

Gesine Sturm and Johannes Bauersachs, *Ich verreise in meinen Garten. Der Garten der Hannah Höch*, Berlin: Stapp, 2007

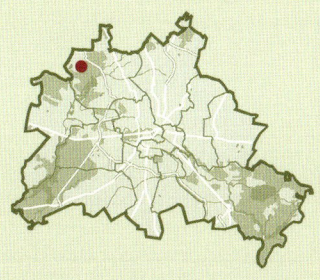

The little exile of Dada's *grande dame*

Diva

advances

A bratwurst in a class of its own—the star of Berlin's snack scene—is the "currywurst." It may be hard to believe, but there's a monument to this sausage drenched in spicy sauce. Since June 2003, a plaque in western Berlin has memorialized Herta Heuwer as the inventor of the currywurst. This Berlin caterer created the recipe for the special curried ketchup as early as 1949, turning the simple bratwurst into Berlin's absolute snack sensation. Ten years later, Heuwer took out a patent on her idea and put the official stamp on her role as the currywurst's originator.

Nowadays you can buy a currywurst anywhere in Germany, and they've even appeared in New York, but the genuine article can only be found in Berlin. Day and night, several hundred stands sell what is probably the city's most popular snack. This sausage is a cult. Politicians and celebrities are addicted to it; it inspired artists (and was the subject of a musical tribute by singer-songwriter Herbert Grönemeyer) and satisfies legions of hungry natives and visitors to the city. The currywurst even made its name as a museum exhibit when Dirk Fellenberg photographed it, as "The Germans' most beloved dish," for the 2006 exhibition *berühmt* ("famous"), and since 2009 the currywurst has even had its own museum in Berlin.

This diva among sausages has also caused some bickering. East and West Berlin squabbled over the ownership of the currywurst. East Berlin always regarded its beloved Konnopke's, a snack bar in Prenzlauer Berg since 1930, with its proprietor Waltraud Ziervogel née Konnopke, as the birthplace of the currywurst, and fiercely defended Konnopke's reputation as its inventor. At Konnopke's, too, the sausage still comes with a sauce based on a secret family recipe. East or West, it tastes fantastic.

Location
Currywurst memorial:
steel plaque at Kantstrasse 101
(facade Kaiser-Friedrich-Strasse)
10627 Berlin

How to get there
U 7 Wilmersdorfer Straße,
S 5, 7, 9 Charlottenburg

Source
www.berlin.de/ba-charlottenburg-wilmersdorf

To find out more
Currywurst Museum, Schützenstrasse 70, 10117 Berlin
Herbert Grönemeyer, "Currywurst," from the album *Total egal*, 1982
www.currybu.de

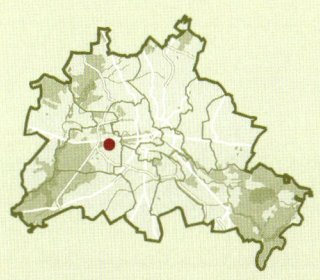

Hier befand sich der Imbiss–Stand,
in dem am 4. September 1949

HERTA HEUWER

30. Juni 1913 in Königsberg – 3. Juli 1999 in Berlin

die pikante Chillup®–Sauce
für die inzwischen weltweit bekannte Currywurst erfand.

Ihre Idee ist Tradition und ewiger Genuss!

Excavating the past

advances

After the war, Berlin lay in ruins. Now that construction work was really dangerous, lacking safety regulations, equipment, and regulated wages, the moment had come to bring in the women (→ Headscarves). But the building site was not the only place where "rubble women" were at work. For a short time, women were permitted to replace fallen or politically compromised men even in leading positions. One was archaeologist Gertrud Dorka (1893–1976), nicknamed "the rubble woman of prehistory." Before the war she had excavated the "Britz Princess," a prehistoric figure buried just outside the city, and in 1947 she was appointed to head Berlin's Museum of Prehistory and Early History, the first woman to be director of a state museum in Germany.

Dorka had waited a good thirty years to be allowed to work in archaeology, a career initially closed to her by her gender. Her university studies had been sacrificed for her brothers' education, and it was by a circuitous route—teaching, attending lectures as a guest auditor, and assisting on excursions and excavations—that she stubbornly worked her way toward her true career goal. In 1936, at over forty years of age, she finally earned her doctorate at the University of Kiel (→ Hungering for knowledge).

Faced with the wartime destruction, the Museum of Prehistory and Early History gratefully accepted Gertrud Dorka's special expertise. The Britz Princess found a new and fitting home at Charlottenburg Palace. Since 2009, the collections of the Museum of Prehistory and Early History have been on display in the New Museum, located on Museum Island.

Nowadays, feminists in Berlin are looking for ways of opening up leadership positions to women *without* the city having to be reduced to ruins first.

Location
Britz Palace,
Alt-Britz 73, 12359 Berlin

How to get there
Bus M 44 Britzer Damm/
Tempelhofer Weg

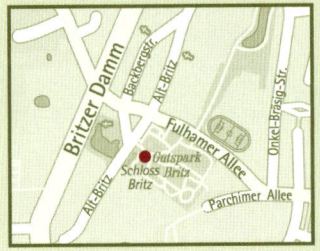

Source

Claudia von Gélieu, *Wegweisende Neuköllnerinnen—von der Britzer Prinzessin zur ersten Stadträtin*, Berlin: trafo, 1998

To find out more

Berlin's equal opportunities legislation: www.berlin.de/sen/frauen/landesdienst/lgg.html

Under the floors of Britz Palace—Berlin's prehistory in women's hands

Fortuna

advances

"What does it take to make a Berlin man happy?" asks a popular melody. The answer: "A summerhouse, a fence, a flower bed" (➤ Paradise). The Berlin woman is harder to please. Her song title of choice is "*Ich will alles—und zwar sofort*": "I want everything—right now." However varied the city's women are, what it takes to make them happy is self-determination, independence, and, of course, true love if possible. Sometimes their personal happiness is completed by children, sometimes not.

But does Berlin make a girl happy? It certainly has a goddess of good luck, who is based, ironically or not, in the problem district of Neukölln. There, in Germany's biggest welfare office, women sit and wait for a little support in their battle against poverty and violence at home or on the streets. Maybe it's here that Fortuna's help is most desperately needed, and here that it's least appropriate to talk of fortune favoring the bold, of people being the architects of their own destiny. To find good fortune you need more than hard work: you need reliable families and quality schools, confidence and social certainties. And especially, as happiness research shows, you need freedom. More than money, love, and personal circumstances, it's freedom from oppression that ensures lasting happiness. The women of Neukölln could tell many a tale about that, not all of them heartwarming. But nothing stops Fortuna in her golden finery from sending her messages of happiness across the district and all of the city. Sometimes it's the little things that make life gleam—the smile of the person sitting opposite you in the metro, a golden buttercup struggling through that crack in the asphalt, the bus driver who sees you running and opens the door, the song of a nightingale heard from the moonlit balcony…

Location
Rathaus Neukölln
(Neukölln Town Hall),
Karl-Marx-Strasse 83, 12043 Berlin

How to get there
U 7 Rathaus Neukölln,
Bus 104, 167 Rathaus Neukölln

To find out more

Institut für europäische Glücksforschung, www.optimalchallenge.com/neu/01.htm

Sonja Lyubomirsky, *Glücklichsein*, Frankfurt: Campus, 2008

Paul Watzlawick, *The Situation Is Hopeless, but Not Serious: The Pursuit of Unhappiness*, New York: Norton, 1983

All that glitters could be gold.

Freedom
advances

"... is always the freedom of the one who thinks differently." The astounding political tolerance these words express was brutally refused to their author, Rosa Luxemburg (1871–1919). The socialist intellectual was beaten and murdered by reactionary Freikorps soldiers on January 15, 1919; her battered body was thrown into the Landwehr Canal.

Rosa Luxemburg, a highly educated Polish Jewish woman who co-founded the Communist Party of Germany, had lived in Berlin since 1899—not on the conventional, bourgeois pattern with husband and children, but in a very modern way: as a professional woman, later divorced, with a housekeeper and visits from her lover. Luxemburg knew how important freedom was for happiness (➤ Fortuna), and she knew how to get it: "Work, that is to say hard, intensive work, which makes complete demands on one's brain and nerves, is, after all, the greatest pleasure in life." This passionate woman was ahead of her time, and ahead of the political dreams of her contemporaries, in many ways. That was the reason she was murdered, the reason she was instrumentalized, and the reason she later became an icon. But none of this takes away from the fact that Rosa Luxemburg reached out and took the freedom she spoke about. And that she described and lived freedom specifically as the freedom of women.

Berlin's women seek that freedom. This city has more women working outside the home than other German towns; it constantly gives rise to new political and feminist impulses. Here women live and love as they please. "Being free means being alone," runs the traditional pop-song philosophy. The anxieties of freedom are supposed to teach us that bitter lesson—but we know better, and refuse to give up the liberty we've won.

Location
Memorial to Rosa Luxemburg on the Landwehr Canal, near Lichtenstein Bridge, Katharina-Heinroth-Ufer, 10787 Berlin

How to get there
S 5, 7 Tiergarten,
Bus 100, 187 Lützowplatz

To find out more

Rosa Luxemburg, dir. Margarethe von Trotta, Germany 1986

Heinz Knobloch, *Meine liebste Mathilde. Die beste Freundin der Rosa Luxemburg*, Frankfurt: Fischer Taschenbuch, 1997

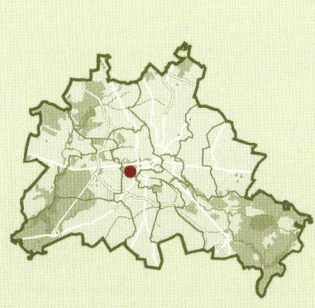

Today it's a peaceful spot between park and zoo.

Golden girl

advances

A well-known German fairy-tale character is the meek and industrious "Golden Marie," who helps out Mother Holle and is rewarded by being covered in gold. But Berlin's "golden girl" is a different matter, looking back on a warrior past. Built in 1873 as the allegorical Victoria atop the Victory Column, she celebrated the wars that Prussia had won against Denmark, Austria, and France, in the wake of which the German Empire came into existence. The era of Kaiser Wilhelm banned women from assembling and of course from voting. It brought a civil code that placed women under male tutelage in every phase of their life, a militaristic cult of masculinity, and ultimately a world war that left women to the exhaustion of the armaments factory and the hardships of starvation on the home front. It was not, then, a very happy period for women—and the gleaming gold of Victoria's robes did nothing to change that. It's not surprising that the famously irreverent Berlin vernacular soon gave the statue its mocking name of *Goldelse*, or "Golden Lizzie."

The Victory Column or *Siegessäule* now has a very unwarlike twin. *Siegessäule* is also the name of the city's gay and lesbian free monthly magazine, ironically standing up for the victorious advance of tolerance and diversity.

Location
Siegessäule (Victory Column), Grosser Stern, 10785 Berlin

How to get there
U 9 Hansaplatz,
Bus 100, 106, 187 Grosser Stern

To find out more
www.siegessaeule.de
http://de.wikipedia.org/wiki/
  E._Marlitt
http://de.wikisource.org/wiki/
  Goldelse

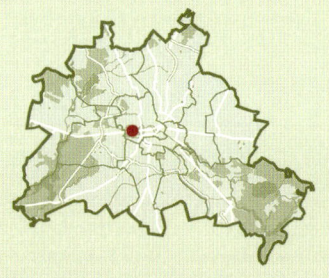

The Prussians surely weren't thinking of victory over intolerance and homophobia.

High above the clouds

advances

"Fly. I wanted to learn to fly. That was absolutely the only thing I knew I wanted," Hedwig Amalie Beese (1886–1925) is said to have commented later in life. The daughter of a wealthy family and a trained sculptor, she took to wearing men's trousers before Marlene Dietrich did (→ Lola), and became famous as Melli Beese, the first woman in Germany to earn a pilot's license for motorized airplanes. To complete the necessary training, she had to overcome every conceivable hurdle. Crash landings and serious injuries, sabotage by male colleagues fearing for their vanity, and extra-rigorous exam conditions all failed to prevent this young woman from obtaining her pilot's license on her twenty-fifth birthday. The same year, she set a new world record at the Berlin-Johannisthal airfield, known as the birthplace of German aviation, for her endurance flight of two hours and nine minutes. The press was jubilant: "Hats off! What that little lady has managed in her Rumpler Taube would be a credit to many of her male colleagues."

In 1912, Melli Beese not only founded her own flying school, but also built and sold her own airplanes. This feisty woman registered several patents: for a collapsible plane, a flying boat, and a single-seat light aircraft. But by 1914 the euphoria of the early years had already faded. When the German Empire declared war on France, the law made Melli Beese—who was married to a Frenchman—officially an enemy of Germany. From then on, her life took an unstoppable tragic turn. In 1925, the once magnificent pilot committed suicide.

Location
Melli-Beese-Strasse,
at the nature preserve on the
former Johannisthal airfield,
Berlin-Adlershof Science
and Technology Park,
S-Bahn Adlershof

How to get there
S 45, 8, 9 Adlershof

Source

"Frauen in Naturwissenschaft und Technik," exhibition curated by the Lübeck University of Applied Sciences, 2008

To find out more

Evelyn Zegenhagen, *"Schneidige deutsche Mädel." Fliegerinnen zwischen 1918 und 1945*, Göttingen: Wallstein, 2007

Takeoffs now from Schönefeld Airport.

Hungering for knowledge

advances

"Books are the stuff of life" announces the neon sign above a bookshop in Prenzlauer Berg. Nowadays, the nourishment of books is accessible to everyone. But women had to travel a long and difficult road before they were allowed to read whatever they wanted. Marie von Ebner-Eschenbach put it in a nutshell: "When a woman learned to read, women's issues entered the world." How true. Reading women create spaces of their own, gaining self-awareness and reflecting on their environment and the condition of their lives. They break through everyday constraints and escape from the authority of men in family and public life. Knowledge and education make women independent and demanding—qualities that irk many men even today. Girls and women now take it for granted that they can satisfy their hunger for education and their thirst for knowledge: at school, where girls generally earn better grades than boys; in vocational training, at college and university, professional training, or night school; in scholarship or research; in politics and administration. Though women are still underrepresented in positions of power, it's no longer possible to imagine their absence.

A century ago, women were involved in education mainly as teachers, librarians, or artists, but today their aspiration for knowledge knows no bounds. And they find unusual ways of passing knowledge on to one another. Take the *Bücherbaum* near Kollwitz Square. Women can find or leave prose, poetry, and nonfiction in this "book tree," a book exchange of a very special kind and free of any financial interest. The idea of "BookCrossing" is now a worldwide movement, encouraging people to leave books they have read to be picked up, free, by others on the public street.

Examples of Berlin women in the recent past who have fed their hunger for education against all the odds are Gertrud Dorka (1893–1976), an educationist and archaeologist, first director of Berlin's Museum of Prehistory and Early History (➤ **Excavating the past**); Melli Beese (1886–1925), sculptor and aviation pioneer, first woman in Germany to earn a pilot's license (➤ **High above the clouds**); Helene Nathan (1885–1940), librarian and director of the municipal library in Neukölln; Käte Frankenthal (1889–1976), doctor, local politician, and municipal physician (➤ **Facts of life**); Katharina Heinroth (1897–1989), animal behaviorist and first female director of the Berlin zoo.

Location
Bücherbaum, Sredskistrasse
at Kollwitzstrasse, 10435 Berlin

How to get there
Tram M 10 Husemannstrasse
U 2 Eberswalder Strasse

Sources
www.luise-berlin.de
www.baufachfrau-berlin.de

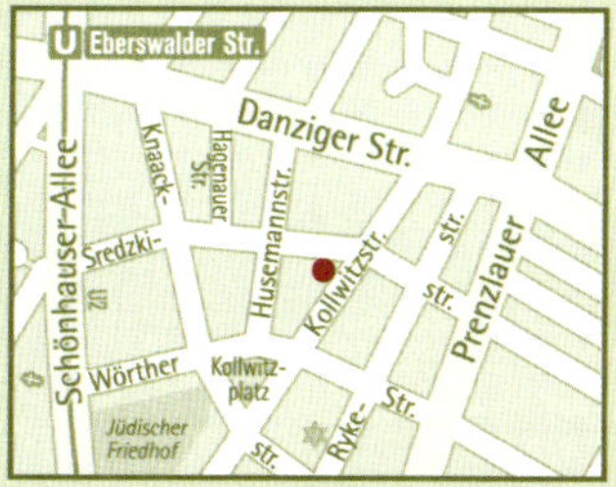

To find out more
Cornelia Carsten et al., *Immer den Frauen nach!* Berlin: Berliner Geschichtswerkstatt, 1993
Claudia von Gélieu, *Wegweisende Neuköllnerinnen*, Berlin: trafo, 1998
Historiale e.V./Bezirksamt Mitte von Berlin (eds), *Frauen in Berlins Mitte*, Berlin: Berlin Story, 2007
Stefan Bollmann, *Women Who Read Are Dangerous*, trans. Christine Shuttleworth, London: Merrell, 2008

Books are the stuff of life, especially for women.

Mount Rubble

advances

The typical Berlin mix of sassiness and self-mockery (➤ Big mouth, big heart) gave birth to this satirical nickname, among so many others. There's not much Alpine about any of the "mountains" in Friedrichshain, Marienhöhe, Rixdorf. They are in fact heaps of ruins and debris deposited after World War II—but despite their high-flown names like Rudöwer Höhe, Insulaner, and Teufelsberg, the locals dubbed all of them Mont Klamott, roughly "Mount Rubble." And they all keep alive the memory of the legendary "rubble women" of Berlin, who shoveled up millions of cubic meters of wreckage to secure their own survival and the survival of the city (➤ Headscarves).

Tamara Danz, lead singer of the East German rock band Silly, celebrated the Mont Klamott of Friedrichshain's public park in an eponymous song. Friedrichshain has two mountains of this kind, officially known as the Small and Large Bunker Mountain, and like almost all the wreckage-based hills in Berlin they are used as parks today. Looking at the peaceful scenes with the neo-bourgeois families of this flourishing neighborhood, gay and lesbian park parties, and relaxed youth culture, it's impossible to guess at the misery of the bunkers and ruins that lies beneath them.

The plateau of the Large Bunker Mountain was the setting for some scenes in the East German cult film *The Legend of Paul and Paula* (DEFA, 1973). The film follows a young mother's individual rebellion against the conventions of socialist society, yet always within the age-old story of how every woman's dream is finding the love of her life. The film's popularity reveals a lot about the gender fantasies behind East Germany's claims to have achieved women's equality. By the way, the beautiful views across the city seen in the film are now obscured by vegetation.

Location

Friedrichshain public park, between Strasse am Friedrichshain, Kniprodstrasse, Danziger Strasse, Landsberger Allee, and Friedenstrasse, 10405 Berlin

How to get there

Tram M 4 Am Friedrichshain, M 10 Kniprodestrasse, M 5, 6 Platz der Vereinten Nationen, Bus 100 Bötzowstrasse

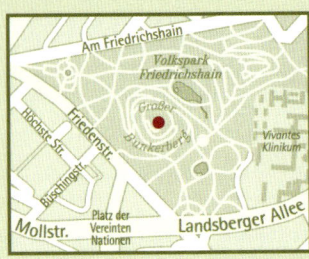

Source

Hans Prang and Günter Kleinschmidt, *Durch Berlin zu Fuß*, East Berlin: Tourist, 1983

Berlin's Alpine landscapes—built from rubble

Queens

advances

In traditional history books (→ Clio), they are usually mentioned only as the wives of the kings of Prussia, their prime task being to secure the royal succession. Yet queens often played an important role in politics, diplomacy, and culture. Some of them left particularly remarkable traces.

The philosopher queen: Sophie Charlotte of Hanover (1668–1705)
Sophie Charlotte was a highly educated, open-minded, and independent woman. Lietzenburg Palace, today known as Charlottenburg Palace, was built under her direction as a home for the intellect and the muses, a gathering place for renowned scholars, philosophers, free thinkers, and artists. She maintained a close lifelong friendship with the polymath Gottfried Wilhelm Leibniz. The establishment of the Prussian Academy of Sciences can be largely credited to her.

The administrator queen: Elisabeth Christine of Brunswick-Wolfenbüttel (1715–1797)
From 1740 onwards, Schönhausen Palace was Elisabeth Christine's main residence. She held court there, arranging concerts, receptions, and discussions. A talented organizer with solid business skills, she administered her estates herself. She commissioned reforestation projects and founded the colony of Schönholz near her palace, providing houses and gardens for migrants from Bohemia. Elisabeth Christine was a pioneer of long-term economic planning and administration.

Location
Schönhausen Palace,
Tschaikowskistrasse 1,
13156 Berlin

How to get there
S 2, 8, 9, U 2 Pankow,
Bus 107, 250 Tschaikowskistrasse

The beauties of administration—Schönhausen Palace in Pankow

Queens *advances*

The middle-class queen: Luise of Mecklenburg-Strelitz (1776–1810)
Luise was brought up in a plainspoken and unconventional way by her grandmother, a follower of the German Enlightenment. That's probably why she constantly broke royal protocol—to the outrage of the whole Prussian court. Her marriage with Friedrich Wilhelm III followed the new bourgeois pattern. The couple addressed each other in the familiar "du" form, the children grew up with their parents, and the family felt most comfortable staying at the modest manor house at Paretz, near Potsdam. Luise's zeal for education, her interest in literature, and her open-minded politics were alien to the King, however. Unlike him, she advocated reform of the underdeveloped German state and tried—in vain—to persuade her husband to support it too.

The charitable queen: Augusta of Saxe-Weimar-Eisenach (1811–1890)
Augusta grew up at the court of Weimar, considered one of the most liberal in Germany, and received a thorough education. Her husband, Wilhelm I of Prussia, sometimes took offence at her astute and lively mind. She was interested in politics and abhorred war. That attitude fueled her many charitable activities, such as founding hospitals and a women's association providing care for wounded and sick soldiers, as well as generous donations to the public soup kitchens. Even becoming empress didn't stop her making regular visits to the soup kitchens (→ Soup-kitchen Lina).

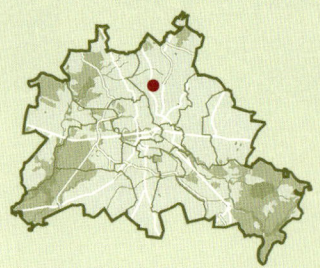

Sources

Renate Feyl, *Aussicht auf bleibende Helle. Die Königin und der Philosoph*, Cologne: Kiepenheuer & Witsch, 2006

Paul Noack, *Elisabeth Christine und Friedrich der Große. Ein Frauenleben in Preußen*, Stuttgart: Klett-Cotta, 2001

Beate Neubauer, "… eine Fürstin, die nie vom Pfade der Tugend abgewichen …," in *SpurenSuche. Frauen in Pankow, Prenzlauer Berg und Weißensee*, Berlin: Bezirksamt Pankow von Berlin, 2006

Günter de Bruyn, *Preußens Luise. Vom Entstehen und Vergehen einer Legende*, Berlin: Siedler, 2001

Heinz Knobloch, *Die Suppenlina. Wiederbelebung einer Menschenfreundin*, Berlin: Edition Hentrich, 1997

To find out more

Beate Neubauer, "Die Kluge, die Schöne, die Vergessenen – Die Königinnen Preußens," in *Loben Sie mich als Frau … Berliner Frauengeschichte erzählt*, Claudia von Gélieu and Beate Neubauer, Berlin: Berlin Edition, 2001

Beate Neubauer, *Hexenküchen, Schlösser & Salons. Geschichten aus dem alten Berlin*, Berlin 2011.

Salon *advances*

Berlin's salons were places that breathed life into the Enlightenment notion of a society of equals and the Romantic ideal of cultivation through conversation. The salon drew together men and women, Jews and Christians, nobility and bourgeoisie. The rigid etiquette of social life was suspended for a few hours, and the emphasis was on personal encounters. This playground for experimentation would later give rise to modernity and democracy, and the way was prepared by women, often Jewish women, whose sex and religion faced them with a double exclusion. These women—the best known today are probably Rahel Varnhagen and Henriette Herz—were educated, but they had no institution or other space where they could bring their social and intellectual skills to bear. In their salons, they created a conversational culture of extraordinary openness and informality. The salon's hospitality did not revolve around food and drink: mostly only tea and cookies were offered. Money was often tight, but the need to discuss art, literature, and politics was urgent.

Intellectual exchange including women, crossing class boundaries and controlled by women themselves, was a novelty that has retained its fascination across the centuries. The renaissance of the salon in today's Berlin is impossible to miss; public, semipublic, and private salons come and go and in some cases seem to be here to stay. The reading group, meeting to talk about literary or scholarly texts, is a form of the salon particularly popular among women. It seems that the blend of personal bonds and intellectual freedom remains a cherished component of democratic education and conviviality.

Location
Literaturhaus,
Fasanenstrasse 23, 10719 Berlin

How to get there
U 1 Uhlandstrasse

Sources
Silvio Vietta (ed.), *Das literarische Berlin im 20. Jahrhundert*, Stuttgart: Philipp Reclam Junior, 2001

Herbert Scurla, *Rahel Varnhagen*, Frankfurt: Fischer Taschenbuch, 1980

To find out more
www.salonkultur.de
Cornelia Saxe, *Das gesellige Canapé. Die Renaissance der Berliner Salons*, Berlin: Quadriga, 1999
www.buecherfrauen.de

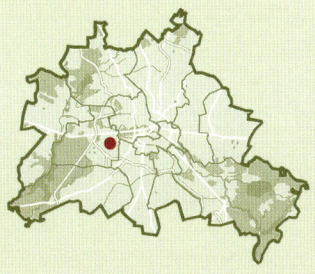

The idea of a democratic public sphere took shape in the salons of Berlin's Enlightenment women.

Second Life

advances

Hopes upon hopes of eternity. In the heavenly paradise, the happy hunting grounds, or Nirvana. In resurrection, even if only as a toad or a dog (→ Dogs). In the arms of the Virgin or with seven virgins in your arms. In seven generations, or at least in one's own children. Maybe in great works of poetry, music, or painting. Maybe in statecraft. Perhaps as the founder of a religion. Or through crime—the more heinous the better; a killing spree at least. The only thing that counts is to continue living, live again. Second Life. The Internet as an immortality machine. Undeletable.

The heavenly realms are uncertain terrain in every faith. What if they don't exist? And if heaven is built on the same patriarchal lines as the religions that proclaim it, it may not sound particularly enticing.

Posthumous fame in the collective memory is just as unpredictable, and it doesn't last forever, especially as the collective mechanisms for wiping women from memory function with amazing precision. And what about our children? Well ... unfortunately ancestor veneration just isn't one of our greatest cultural skills.

In view of all this, the opportunities for self-documentation through publications, photographs, and especially the Internet offer a relatively gender-democratic medium for keeping women's memories alive. As so often, the principle of do-it-yourself is the modern woman's ultimate multipurpose weapon.

Nietzsche's Zarathustra provided a popular quote for German gravestone inscriptions: "But all joy wants eternity." Maybe women should just turn that around, forget eternity, and take their joy in the here and now.

Location
Alter St.-Matthäus-Kirchhof,
Grossgörschenstrasse 12,
10829 Berlin

How to get there
S 1, 2 Yorckstrasse/
Grossgörschenstrasse,
U 7 Yorckstrasse

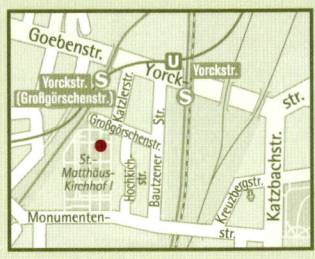

To find out more

www.stiftung-historischefriedhoefe.de
www.grabpatenschaften-berlin.de
www.jugendmuseum.de
Rosemarie Köhler, *Sie lebten wie sie wollten. Berliner Friedhofsspaziergänge zu Grabstätten außergewöhnlicher Frauen*, Berlin: Orlanda, 2006.

Not necessarily all the same in death—queer embellishments on Schöneberg graves

Washing machine

advances

The new Federal Chancellery in Berlin was built on a very, very big scale. Compared with its counterpart in the old capital, Bonn, it exudes an unmistakable will to power and prestige. This imposing building was commissioned by the previous Chancellor Helmut Kohl, built by Charlotte Frank and Axel Schultes (who won the 2003 German Architecture Prize for it), opened by Gerhard Schröder, and since 2005 has been the headquarters of Germany's first woman chancellor, Angela Merkel—though the enormous circles dominating its facades had already earned it the nickname "washing machine" before a woman arrived as the new head of the household.

Women and power—an old and difficult story. The scrap of power that royal women could access by virtue of their noble blood was refused to every woman by bourgeois society: the right to political participation, whether as voter or officeholder. Against that backdrop, it's not surprising that many people automatically think of a male officeholder when they imagine the successful exercise of power. When Merkel took office, a national newspaper regretted that now there would be no one to wave down at the amateur soccer players playing on the lawn in front of the Chancellery, and that this would mean losing some of the affinity between the people and its government. In cases like these, historians talk of the king's two bodies: an immortal body representing royal power, and an ordinary, mortal body that is of no great interest. From that point of view, Chancellor Merkel has actually done everything right. The endless comments about her figure and hairstyle seem to bounce off her like a marble statue, and she has shown that you can govern perfectly well without the prestige function of a male body. Perhaps that's due to a woman's brain.

Location
Federal Chancellery,
Willy-Brandt-Strasse 1,
10557 Berlin

How to get there
U 55 Bundeskanzleramt,
S 5, 7, 9 Hauptbahnhof,
S 1, 2, 25 Brandenburger Tor,
Bus 100 Reichstag / Bundestag

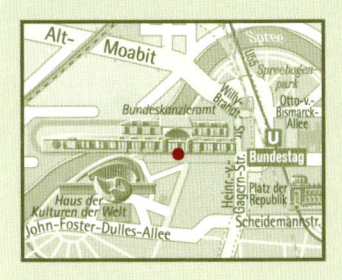

A Federal Chancellery with a woman's touch

HIER WOHNTE
FELICE
SCHRAGENHEIM
JG. 1922
DEPORTIERT 1944
THERESIENSTADT
AUSCHWITZ
GROSS ROSEN

adventures

Lieselotte-Berger-Platz

Elfriede-Kuhr-Str.
10 - 20

Aimée & Jaguar

adventures

They met in the middle of the war under circumstances that could not have been more dramatic. Felice Schragenheim was living illegally, battling her way through a Berlin that in 1942 was at the height of the Nazi power frenzy and had set the course for the final extermination of the Jews. The net of controls was getting ever tighter, informers were working for the Gestapo, and very few people were willing to help the desperate who tried to survive illegally, underground. Then Felice met Lilly Wust, housewife and mother of four, whose husband was a dedicated soldier fighting in the war for Hitler. The two women fell in love. Lilly took in Felice, at first unaware that she was Jewish. Aimée and Jaguar—that's what they called themselves—lived their forbidden love in the eye of the storm. But they were denounced and Felice was deported to the Theresienstadt concentration camp in 1944. Lilly developed unknown strengths; she fought and even went to Theresienstadt to visit her lover. Somewhere, probably on a transport to Bergen-Belsen, Felice died. Lilly kept the story to herself for decades. Her story did not fit into postwar Germany, which sought its footing by repressing Nazism and absorbing itself in petty-bourgeois family life. There was no place for lesbian love.

Up to 7,000 Jews attempted to survive in Berlin as Felice did, underground or in hiding, as so-called U-boats, or submarines (➤ **U-boats**).

Stolpersteine, or stumbling stones, like the one in front of the house where Felice and Lilly had lived, are cobblestones with a brass surface set into the sidewalk. They tell the story of Jews, people in the resistance, homosexuals, Sinti and Roma, or people with disabilities that fell victim to the Nazis.

Location
"Stolperstein" for Felice Schragenheim, Friedrichshaller Strasse 23, 14199 Berlin

How to get there
Bus 110, 186, 249 Berkaer Strasse/Breite Strasse

Sources

Erica Fischer, *Aimée & Jaguar: A Love Story, Berlin 1943*, trans. Edna McCown, Boston: Alyson Books, 1998

Neue Gesellschaft für Bildende Kunst e.V. (ed.), *Stolpersteine. Für die von den Nazis ermordeten ehemaligen Nachbarn aus Friedrichshain und Kreuzberg. Dokumentation, Texte, Materialien*, Berlin: NGBK, 2002

A faint reflection of rescue, love, and betrayal

Berlin flower

adventures

Berliners call a native of their city a "Berlin flower." They mean that robust weed growing between the cracks in the asphalt, quick-witted, never at a loss for words, and the epitome of street credibility (➤ Big mouth, big heart). Like Nina Hagen, whose career took her from quirky pop starlet to mother of punk. In 1976, she hit the world in a whirlwind from East Berlin, a provocation to sleepy guitarists, established rock heroes, and incredulous TV audiences, especially with her TV appearance demonstrating successful masturbation. It would take a lot to match that.

Helga Hahnemann (1937–1991), East Berlin's favorite jokester, was just as outspoken, twisting the knife in the wounds of the socialist republic and the complacent West alike. Affectionately dubbed "The Hen," her name lives on in the German TV award *Goldene Henne* or "Golden Hen."

A very special flower is Désirée Nick, inventor of the "lady joke." With her degree in Catholic theology, classical dance training, and a six-foot stature that ruled her out of dancing for the German Opera, she likes to hold up a mocking feminist mirror to self-satisfied Berliners of every sort. Claire Waldoff was probably the quintessential Berlin flower. She came to the city from the industrial Ruhr in 1906. Quickly mastering Berlin's typical backchat, Claire epitomized the Weimar cabaret scene with her shirt and necktie, brassy red pixie cut, and her girlfriend on her arm. The No. 1 exemplar of the women's libber, she was the undisputed queen of lesbian Berlin. Nobody was quite as impudent as Claire. "Kick the men ➤ Out, out, out of the Reichstag," she demanded, and publicly ridiculed the Nazis in her satirical song "Who's That Chucking Mud?" When they gained power in 1933, of course, she was immediately banned from the stage.

Location
Sculpture on Claire-Waldoff-Platz,
at the Friedrichstadtpalast,
Friedrichstrasse 107,
10117 Berlin

How to get there
S-Bahn/U-Bahn Friedrichstrasse,
U 6 Oranienburger Tor

43

Better a head without a body than a body without a head …

Clio

adventures

Clio, the Muse of history, is the first and most important of the nine Muses, the daughters of Zeus who brought humanity the creative arts. It's too bad she never showed much favor to her mortal sisters. On the contrary, the achievements of women—whether as rulers, poets, or just ordinary women of every era—get forgotten as night follows day; they are belittled and relegated to secondary importance (→ Painting ladies, → Queens). Describing how women constantly fade out of collective memory, Berlin artist Gisela Breitling remarks that it's almost as if their history had been written with some kind of magical, disappearing ink.

For example, when a canon of important literature is put together, the works of women authors are not taken into account. When role models are listed, no women appear. Great women mutate into mere appendages of men or into caricatures drawn by demeaning fantasies. That situation has made it impossible for a tradition to arise where women feel assured of their history. Women's political struggles, in particular, face a special rule of silence. Their role is distorted and treated as ludicrous. The feminists of the 1970s knew nothing about the women who had fought similar battles just a few decades before them; those women's writings and efforts to achieve education, suffrage, and employment had been completely erased from history. Only the dismissive labels "bluestockings" and "suffragettes" found a way into society's collective consciousness.

Looking into an empty mirror is discouraging. That's one reason why writing women's history has become a fundamental concern of feminist historiography and the archives of the women's movement. Clio, we need you!

Location
Statue of Clio at the Nikolaikirche, Nikolaikirchplatz 1, 10178 Berlin

How to get there
S-Bahn/U-Bahn Alexanderplatz, Bus 100, 200 Lustgarten

To find out more
Women's research, education, and information center FFBIZ e.V., Eldenaer Strasse 35 III, 10247 Berlin
Lesbian archive and library Spinnboden: www.spinnboden.de
L'Homme – Europäische Zeitschrift für Feministische Geschichtswissenschaft, Cologne: Böhlau Verlag
www.frauentouren.de

The empty mirror of women's history is filling up with reflections.

Ewa, Frieda, Paula, Marie ...

adventures

The names they chose, EWA (as in "Eve"), Frieda, Mathilde, Paula, or Marie, weren't based on the rankings of Berlin's most popular girls' names. Frieda stands for Friedrichshain, Paula for Pankow, Marie for Marzahn—these were women's spaces set up by politically committed women in East Berlin's districts during the first few months after the Wall came down.

The idea arose in the grassroots groups involved in the roundtables of bodies like the New Forum, the Green League, the Independent Women's League, and the Lutheran church. The founders aimed to create spaces from which women could intervene in politics, participate in the process of building the new Germany, and demand to be taken seriously (➛ Mothers).

The period saw frighteningly rapid social and political change, unemployment, new legal systems, the loss of old values and social frameworks. In that context, the new women's centers became the first point of call for women who felt overwhelmed by the upheaval and needed support. Very soon, information and counseling services were established, along with vocational training and retraining programs. The centers also organized discussion groups where women looked for shared solutions to their everyday problems.

Today, these locations from the early days of united Germany define themselves as sociocultural women's projects, their doors open to unemployed women, mothers, lesbians, migrants, and retirees. They are places for conversation and networking, integration and advice, self-help and mutual support.

Location
EWA Women's Center e.V.,
Prenzlauer Allee 6, 10405 Berlin

How to get there
Tram M 1 Prenzlauer Allee / Metzer Strasse

To find out more
Barbara Hömberg, *Geteilte Schwestern? Probleme in der Zusammenarbeit von Ost- und Westfrauenbewegung unter besonderer Berücksichtigung des EWA e.V.–Frauenzentrums in Berlin-Prenzlauer Berg*, Berlin: Diplomica, 1994

Where dreams grow heavenward …

Headscarves

adventures

At the end of World War II, Berlin urgently needed reconstruction. There were few men around, so it was mainly women who performed the heavy labor of removing the rubble, ash, and debris. Streets had to be cleared, bomb craters filled, unsafe façades demolished. Between 20,000 and 60,000 women and girls, officially called unskilled construction laborers, passed rubble from hand to hand, chipped the mortar from old bricks, salvaged reusable building material, loaded stone and wreckage onto horse-drawn carts, and often pulled those carts themselves. There was little technology to help, just trolley-style locomotives brought from the western coalmines to help carry away the rubble (➤ Mount Rubble). The work was unbelievably hard and dangerous, with frequent accidents due to buildings collapsing or munitions exploding. The wages were food ration cards and thus a chance of survival. When the worst of the work was done, when the men came home, labor got easier, and wage packets fatter, gender roles were restored to normal: in the city's western sector, women were banned from construction work until 1994.

However, the *Trümmerfrau* or "rubble woman" became a founding myth in both East and West Berlin. In the West she sits in Hasenheide park, weary from her work. Perhaps she's looking forward to her coming life as a housewife and mother? In the East she shoulders her shovel—although, please note, *in front of* the Red Town Hall, not *inside* it—and strides boldly toward a glowing future.

What they have in common is the headscarf. Then still free of ideological baggage, the scarf protected women from dirt and rain but also made a subtly localized fashion statement: knotted at the top was considered the urban style, while a knot at the nape was the rural woman's choice.

Location
West: "Trümmerfrau," Hasenheide park, Graefestrasse entrance, 10967 Berlin
East: "Aufbauhelferin," Rathausstrasse at Spandauer Strasse, 10178 Berlin

How to get there
West: U 7 Südstern or Hermannplatz; East: U-Bahn / S-Bahn Alexanderplatz, Tram M 4, M 5, and M 6 Spandauer Strasse

Sources
www.luise-berlin.de
www.stadtentwicklung.berlin.de

To find out more
Die Trümmerfrauen von Berlin, film documentary by Hans-Dieter Grabe, West Germany 1968
http://www.bauhandwerkerinnen.de/geschichte/geschichte.htm

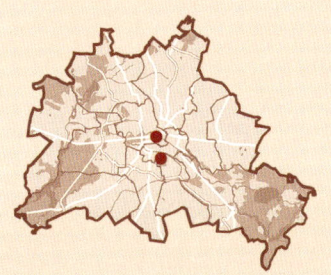

Back when a headscarf was not a political statement

Mothers

adventures

What if we didn't have Article 3 of the German Basic Law—the clear and unequivocal statement "Men and women shall have equal rights"?

There would be no legal basis for sixty years of tenacious struggle for equal rights and opportunities for women, for all the battles over men's legal supremacy in marriage and family, women's exclusion from certain professions, the law on family names, and so on and so forth. Each step has had to be wrested from bitter resistance, yet all this time the simple declaration has been there, permanently undermining every claim of the allegedly natural or divinely ordained difference between the sexes.

That simple, reasonable sentence was itself fiercely controversial. The West German constitution was drafted after the disastrous masculinity cult of the Nazis, after women's incredible work to ensure survival in the shattered cities and psyches of the wartime and postwar years (→ Headscarves). But the much-vaunted "Fathers of the Basic Law" did not think it necessary to give women an equal position in the state—on the contrary. The churches were in full cry, the middle classes longed for the return of the cozy old days, social democracy didn't want to rob the worker of his little bit of power at the family hearth. There was no sign of a lobby for women.

It's social democrat Elisabeth Selbert we have to thank for the ultimate adoption of equal rights in the Basic Law. A member of the Parliamentary Council drawing up the constitution, she proposed the paragraph, which the gentlemen hastened to reject. She first convinced the three other female members of the council, then embarked on a highly publicized trip across the country, visiting women in women's associations, political parties, trade unions, companies, and town councils to mobilize support for her idea. Before long, the story goes, whole laundry baskets full

Location
Volksbühne theater,
Rosa-Luxemburg-Platz,
10178 Berlin

How to get there
U 2 Rosa-Luxemburg-Platz

Where are the mothers of women's equality?

Mothers

adventures

of protest letters were arriving at the council. Lo and behold, the vital sentence was unanimously accepted in January 1949—and the founding fathers of the Basic Law were joined by founding mothers.

The educational effect on men in power was not a lasting one, however. When the Berlin Wall came down and a new constitution was needed for the unified Germany, the mountain labored and brought forth a mouse: the new, improved version ran "Women and men shall have equal rights." This belated act of courtesy wasn't quite enough for the new generation. Their campaign to get women's rights into the constitution, driven primarily by women jurists and local women's and equal-opportunities officers across the country, achieved a success similar to their mothers'. More than 200,000 submissions were made, and Article 3, Paragraph 2 of the Basic Law was supplemented by the sentence: "The state shall promote the actual implementation of equal rights for women and men and take steps to eliminate disadvantages that now exist."

One of the precursors of this campaign was the women's congress held on December 3, 1989, at the Volksbühne theater in Berlin. Hardly had the Wall come down than East German women met to draft a manifesto for an autonomous women's movement, under the banner "No new state without women." The resulting Independent Women's League, UFV, was a political voice bringing the experiences of East German women to the unified Republic.

There is no automatic mechanism for achieving women's rights, as women continue to find out to their cost. That means there'll always be a need for the mothers, daughters, and granddaughters of the Basic Law.

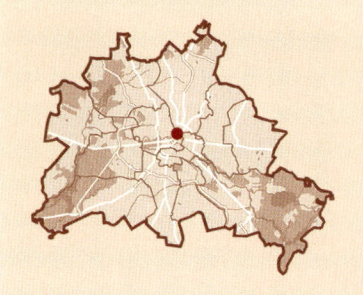

Sources
"Elisabeth Selbert," in *Wegweiserinnen*, ed. Stadt Lünen, Gleichstellung – Frauenbüro, City of Lünen, 2002
www.fembio.org/biographie.php/frau/biographie/elisabeth-selbert

To find out more
Florence Hervé and Renate Wurms (eds), *Das Weiberlexikon. Von Abenteurerin bis Zyklus*, Cologne: Papyrossa, 2006
Women's library and archive "HexLibris – Frauenbibliothek & Archiv des EWA e.V.– Frauenzentrum," www.ewa-frauenzentrum.de

Neighborhood moms

adventures

The media dub them "supernannies" or the "Mom SWAT," but the mothers organizing locally take a much more down-to-earth view of themselves and their advocacy work. As one of them put it modestly, "Neighborhood moms learn what they can, and pass on what they've learned to families with an immigration background."

Where the well-paid, highly trained experts in schools and kindergartens, municipal offices, youth clubs, and neighborhood management projects have failed, the moms are called in. Six months of training in childcare, health promotion, German language and law—and these mothers and grandmothers of Turkish or Arab origin are entrusted with the task of saving their neighborhoods from ghettoization and educational collapse. At least, nowadays, they receive a nominal fee.

The pilot project "Neighborhood Mothers in Neukölln" was launched in 2004 by the Lutheran social service agency. It now has around 150 mothers, and other districts are following suit. The project was awarded the German integration prize and Berlin's crime prevention prize, and it was probably due to these women that Neukölln was chosen for the European Union "Intercultural Cities" program in 2008, the only German municipality selected.

Like other mothers, neighborhood moms can do anything. They open doors that social workers don't even knock on. They build confidence. They encourage healthy eating and exercise. They pass on tips on childrearing, language classes, or negotiating the bureaucratic jungle, and aren't afraid to tackle issues such as domestic violence or sexuality. If these women didn't exist, they'd have to be invented very fast. As they do exist, they ought to be paid adequately. And maybe they should give lessons to some of those "integration" professionals (➔ Multiculti).

Location
International kitchen
"WARThE MAhL,"
Warthestrasse 45/46,
12051 Berlin

How to get there
S 41, 42, 46, 47,
U 8 Hermannstrasse

Sources
Daily newspapers
dbb magazin, December 2006

Countering the dangers of marginalization

55

Public money

adventures

Women need money, women's projects need money, and there never seems to be enough of it under women's control. For many years, the wide range of projects and initiatives that arose from the second-wave women's movement, starting from the 1970s, had to live on love alone—along with a seemingly endless supply of unpaid commitment.

Yet wasn't it the women's movement that declared war on the invisible, unpaid, and unappreciated work of women? Wasn't the important work of feminist projects worth paying for? Wasn't society as a whole responsible for women's shelters, training, help in returning to employment? Why not demand that the state fulfill its responsibility for an equitable society?

To this end, in 1980 a task force was formed to promote independent women's projects, citizens' initiatives, and alternative projects. Its tongue-in-cheek name was *AK Staatsknete*, the "public dough committee." Heated debates over autonomy and co-option surrounded the group, which brought together more than forty women's projects—anything from archives to shelters to training programs—in a single feminist network. *AK Staatsknete* was dissolved in 1998, but it left behind a series of successful spin-off projects, some of them still pillars of feminist politics in today's Berlin. Examples are the funding network for women's projects *Goldrausch* (➛ **Gold rush**) and ZOFF, the "campaign for the future of women," which aims to create jobs for unemployed women university graduates. In fact, the ruinous banking scandal that hit Berlin at the turn of the 21st century raised the question whether government money wouldn't be generally better off in women's hands.

Location
Berliner Frauenbund 1945 e.V.,
Ansbacher Strasse 63,
10777 Berlin

How to get there
U 3, 9 Spichernstrasse,
U 4 Viktoria-Luise-Platz

Source

http://www.ffbiz.de/htdocs/
content/Suchlisteberlin.pdf

"Grandparent Service" at the Berlin Women's League

Showtime

adventures

Berlin's greatest theatrical woman was certainly Helene Weigel—they say even God lined up at the box office of the radical theater Berliner Ensemble to see her. But He wasn't the audience she had in mind. As an actor and the Ensemble's artistic director, she made German theatrical history between 1949 and her death in 1971. With her husband Bertolt Brecht, she worked for a new, socialist form of theater that broke with bourgeois tradition.

Before and after Weigel, Berlin's theaters have seen countless outstanding actresses: Marlene Dietrich and Marianne Hoppe, Angela Winkler and Angelica Domröse, Nina Hoss and Fritzi Haberlandt, Katharina Schüttler and Sophie Rois, to name just a few.

Women in charge seem to be a cultural challenge in theater as everywhere else. The male domain of directing is increasingly being conquered by women: Andrea Breth at Berlin's Schaubühne; Karin Henkel, now at Vienna's Burgtheater but for many years at the Berliner Ensemble and the Volksbühne; Sasha Waltz with exciting dance at the Schaubühne and the Radialsystem arts space; Shermin Langhoff with her intercultural experimentalism at Ballhaus Naunynstrasse; Constanze Behrens with her witty productions at the Prime Time Theater, tucked away at the theatrical margins in working-class Wedding; and many more.

The nonprofit Theater Eigenreich, housed in a former textile factory on Greifswalder Strasse and headed by Verena Drosner, offers a forum for young female playwrights. And the new generation of theatrical women is safely on its way: at Berlin's Ernst Busch College of Performing Arts alone, women currently make up around half those studying stage direction and 40 percent of student actors.

Location
Berliner Ensemble,
Schiffbauerdamm,
Bertolt-Brecht-Platz 1,
10117 Berlin

How to get there
S-Bahn/U-Bahn Friedrichstrasse

Sources
www.hfs-berlin.de
www.berliner-ensemble.de

To find out more
Current calendar of the Berlin theaters
www.ballhausnaunynstrasse.de
www.eigenreich-berlin.de
www.primetimetheater.de

The Berliner Ensemble. How much of Brecht is actually Weigel?

Splitting the atom

adventures

"Everything about this woman seemed simple but exquisite. I remember well how L. and E. tried to impress her. It was amusing, almost bizarre ... as if two high-school students were competing for the attention of a girl. In fact, all three were over fifty years old."

The high-school students were Nobel prizewinners Albert Einstein and Max von Laue, and the girl was physicist Lise Meitner, who made an immense scientific contribution to nuclear fission in collaboration with the chemist Otto Hahn. To be sure, it was Hahn who received the Nobel Prize for their work; Meitner's work remained unrecognized (➔ **Clio**).

The Austrian Lise Meitner (1878–1968) passed her college entrance exam at 22, having had to study alone because girls were excluded from higher schooling. After studying physics, mathematics, and philosophy, she was only the second woman to gain a Ph.D. at the University of Vienna. She moved to Berlin, attended Max Planck's lectures, and met Otto Hahn, with whom she would work for the next thirty years. She became a pioneering nuclear physicist and was soon causing a scientific stir.

In 1907 she was refused entry to her male colleagues' most important laboratories, and couldn't use the Institute's main entrance. In the 1920s, however, her career took off thanks to her outstanding research work, and in 1922 she became the first woman physicist to be awarded her full university teaching qualification. In 1926 she was appointed professor extraordinarius— that is, an unpaid professor—of experimental nuclear physics in Berlin. When Hitler took power, her license to teach was revoked. Exiled in Sweden, she continued working on the theoretical interpretation of nuclear fission and early recognized its dangerous potential. All her life, she refused to work on the atomic bomb.

Location
Plaque commemorating Lise Meitner's workplace, Otto Hahn Building, Free University Berlin, Thielallee 63, 14195 Berlin

How to get there
U 3 Thielplatz

Source
Michael Grüning, *Ein Haus für Albert Einstein. Erinnerungen, Briefe, Dokumente*, Berlin: Verlag der Nation, 1990

They split the atom—but they didn't split the Nobel Prize.

U-boats

adventures

When the Nazis banned emigration in October 1941, Germany became a deadly trap for all Jews still living there. The only way of escaping deportation was to go underground. In Berlin, up to 7,000 Jews tried to evade the grip of the Gestapo as "U-boats"—or submarines, people hiding in the city or surviving with false identities (➤ **Aimée & Jaguar**).

That was possible only with the courageous help of many non-Jews who hid the persecuted in their apartments or summerhouses, found them forged papers, passed them food, or even helped them across the border. The exact number of people who resisted the fascist regime as "silent helpers" is unknown. In most cases, several people were involved in a rescue, and the people in hiding usually had to change their shelter many times.

What we do know is that women made up around two thirds of the helpers who assisted Jews living in Germany between 1941 and 1945. Very few of those women's names are known to us today. Helene von Schell, Kläre Bloch, Helene Jacobs, Hildegard Jacoby, Hildegard Schaeder, Gertrud Staewen, Melanie Steinmetz, Maria Nickel, Wanda Feuerherm—these women must stand in for the many who helped Jews in Berlin for all sorts of different reasons. They were taking a high personal risk: a Nazi decree had declared contact with Jews to be a criminal act. The punishments were unpredictable, and could range from official warnings and fines, to jail or penal servitude, to being sent to a concentration camp.

The stories of these helpers belie later claims made by many Germans: firstly that no one knew about the persecution, and secondly that no resistance to the Nazi regime was possible.

Location
Memorial plaque for
Helene von Schell,
Waldstrasse 6, 10551 Berlin

How to get there
Bus TXL, 106, 107
Turmstrasse / Beusselstrasse

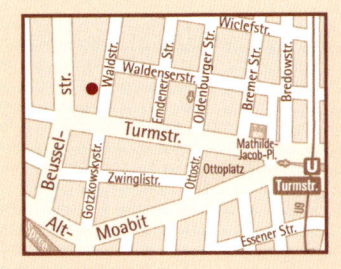

Source

Beate Kosmala, *Verbotene Hilfe. Rettung für Juden in Deutschland 1941–1945* (vol. 56 of *Gesprächskreis Geschichte*), Bonn: Friedrich Ebert Foundation, 2004

To find out more

Silent Heroes Memorial Center—Resistance to Persecution of the Jews 1933–1945, exhibition and catalog (both in English), Rosenthaler Strasse 39, 10178 Berlin

BERLINER GEDENKTAFEL

In diesem Hause lebte

HELENE VON SCHELL

20. 7. 1903 – 4. 3. 1956

Während der NS-Herrschaft versteckte sie hier in ihrer Wohnung eine vierköpfige jüdische Familie die sie unter Lebensgefahr vor der Deportation und Ermordung bewahrte

Islands of courage and humanity

ÜPFI

adventures

You could be forgiven for thinking that the old slogan "Together, women are strong" has been well and truly forgotten as women try to fight their way through the glass ceiling. But there's an exception. Two high-ranking women politicians, from different parties, met one day on the stairs of Berlin's House of Representatives, and realized they had had just about enough of endless, unproductive debates. Their frustration and derision gave birth to the idea of starting up a new form of politics, setting off on a new path.

That was the background of the new body formed in 1992, the ÜPFI or "Cross-party Women's Initiative Berlin—City of Women," a coalition of politically active women from all parties. No doubt the experience garnered at the ➤ **Witches' breakfast** played its part. At any rate, the organization's objective was (and still is) to take shared insights, information, and good political ideas and turn them into productive action. It was an audacious attempt at collaboration between women that ignored party boundaries to further a feminist agenda. It soon gathered momentum, joined by women's issues specialists from all the parties and by other women—from the federal parliament, Berlin's administration, and nongovernmental women's projects, associations, and media. When the notables of gender policy in Berlin gather at ÜPFI's exuberant New Year's reception every year, the success of this networking becomes abundantly clear.

Location
Berlin House of Representatives,
Niederkirchnerstrasse 3–5,
10117 Berlin

How to get there
S-Bahn / U-Bahn Potsdamer Platz,
Bus 200, 347 Potsdamer Platz,
U 2 Mohrenstrasse

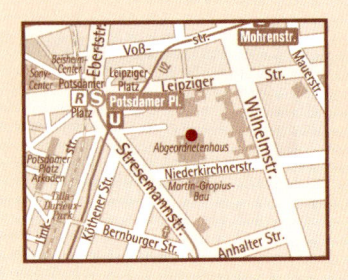

Sources
www.berlin-stadtderfrauen.de
www.lernhaus-berlin.de

Children's sink in the women's restroom, House of Representatives

Witches' breakfast

adventures

Think back to a time when the Berlin Wall was still standing, when Green Party participation in a coalition government still seemed an act of unheard-of audacity, when West Berlin's government had neither a Minister for Women's Affairs nor any other recognition of the importance of women's issues. In 1989, the Social Democrat/Green coalition's appointment of women to head eight of the city government's thirteen departments caused a sensation. One of these was responsible for women's affairs, and she was also Berlin's first openly lesbian political office-holder (Anne Klein, 1950–2011). In their previous political lives, these eight women had gathered enough experience to know the truth in the saying "United we stand, divided we fall." They put that into practice in the shape of an informal, innovative, and cross-party institution called the Witches' Breakfast. The name was an ironic allusion to the demonization of strong women and the male anxieties that fuel it. It wasn't just the name that made men suspicious, though: the breakfast was a successful strategy for implementing women's political objectives. Berlin's pathbreaking equal-opportunities legislation is one of the fruits of this collective effort. The strength of the "women's Senate" of 1989–1991 was also fed by mutual support in a turbulent era of kindergarten strikes, political infighting, and the fall of the Wall.

Location
Schöneberg Town Hall,
John-F.-Kennedy-Platz,
10825 Berlin

How to get there
U 4, Bus 104 Rathaus Schöneberg

How men get a handle on power

Woman of the Year Award

adventures

When the great poet Friedrich Schiller honored women for weaving heavenly roses into life's mundanity, a parodist responded that women should indeed be honored—because they knit such cozy socks. Of course, sock-knitting is a wonderful thing, especially in an era when a gift of handmade knitwear has become such a rare pleasure.

Even so, acknowledging their knitting skills really isn't giving women the honor they deserve, and that is why almost every year since 1988, the city of Berlin has presented the *Frauenpreis*, its Woman of the Year Award. The prize honors a Berlin woman who, to put it in poetic terms, took up arms for the liberty of her sex, or, as the bureaucrats phrase it more soberly, made an active contribution to gender equality and women's emancipation. The difficult part of this award is picking just one woman out of the huge number who are at work on women's issues across the city. They might be based in a grassroots project in the Wedding district or at the elite university in Dahlem, in an established association or a spontaneous initiative, be a real → Berlin flower or one of the Berliners-at-heart who have come here from all over the world (bearing in mind that from the Berliner's point of view, the world begins—or ends—at most ten miles from Alexanderplatz). One thing's for sure: Berlin has no lack of magnificent, committed women.

The prize includes a little money and, more importantly, a lot of elation and celebration, drawing hundreds to the International Women's Day festivities in the Red Town Hall on March 8 each year. The Town Hall's Louise Schroeder Auditorium, named after the only female governing mayor Berlin has had so far, is too small for the party, but all the better: it's nice to see the entire Town Hall taken over by women.

Location
Rotes Rathaus (Red Town Hall),
Rathausstrasse 15, 10178 Berlin

How to get there
U-Bahn / S-Bahn Alexanderplatz,
Tram M 4, M 5, M 6 Spandauer Strasse

To find out more
http://www.berlin.de/rbmskzl/
ehrungen/index.html#
louiseschroeder

Women keeping their eyes on the prize

Women's quarter

adventures

"The whiff of indecency, the seedy red glow, the dark shadows of love for sale—no, absolutely no: Neukölln must remain unsoiled! Neukölln already has a reputation as the 'end of the line,' but the Christian Democratic Union's courageous resolution will avert the added stigma of its sounding like a red-light quarter. The new district on the Rudower Felder will not, as the feminists have demanded, be called 'Women's Quarter,' but instead 'Garden City Rudow.' The sex-trade associations have now been warded off." This was the commentary of Berlin's local paper *Tagesspiegel* in summer 1998.

Yet that same year, after much debate and against dogged resistance, all twenty streets and squares of a newly built neighborhood in the southeast of Neukölln were named after women. For the first time, Berlin had a real "women's quarter."

In fact, a century earlier the streets of a neighborhood in Höhenschönhausen, northeastern Berlin, had been given girls' names—Elsastrasse, Annemariestrasse, and so on. But the intended effect was to stress the sweetness and charm of this residential area around a little lake. The Neukölln activists had a very different aim: to honor women's work and achievements. These streets bear the names of women who stood up socially and politically for women's rights and equality, women who resisted the Nazis, women who worked for a democratic and peaceful Germany after the war. The controversy around red-light districts still rages in Neukölln—but nowadays the issue is brothels (→ Red-light).

Location
"Women's quarter,"
Lieselotte-Berger-Strasse at
Elfriede-Kuhr-Strasse,
12355 Berlin

How to get there
Bus 171 Lieselotte-Berger-Strasse,
Bus 371 Lieselotte-Berger-Platz

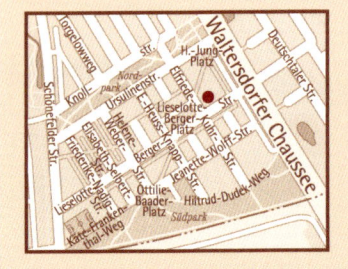

Source

20 Jahre Frauen-/Gleichstellungsbeauftragte, brochure published by the Berlin Senate's Department of Women's Issues, Berlin 2006

A whole district full of women, and not a single red lamp

Alte Liebe

"Leise, Peterle, leise, der Mond geht auf die Reise..."

emotions

BABYLON

MUHE ANTONIONI PLENZDORF

Anne and her three husbands

emotions

It's not something you might have expected to find in biblical history: the veneration of a woman who married three times, remained childless for many years, and only at an advanced age gave birth to a daughter, joined later by half-brothers from two further marriages. This was a real "patchwork family," and its second generation also took an unusual turn, featuring the immaculate conception of the founder of a religion. The father in that story, far from entering the religious history books as a paragon of socially aware fatherhood, has been marginalized, even smirked at, in popular understanding.

That wasn't always the case. Even if some representatives of the Church tried to create the impression that the patriarchal unit—breadwinner father, housewife mother, and as large as possible a brood of children—is the prototype of the Christian family, that's not only historically shortsighted, but also contradicts the biblical story itself. There we find memorable role models for a touching family community including Mary's mother Anne; Anne's husbands Joachim, Cleophas, and Salomas; Mary, Joseph, Jesus, and John his half-brother. The Lutheran privileging of marriage as the form of life most pleasing to God played an important part in wiping the tradition of the Holy Kinship from our visual memory.

In 1505, Tilman Riemenschneider carved the group "Saint Anne and Her Three Husbands" in lime wood. You can find it in the Bode Museum in Berlin. Good news for secular Berlin!

Location
Bode Museum, Museum Island,
Bodestrasse 1, 10117 Berlin

How to get there
S 1, 2 Oranienburger Strasse,
S 5, 7, 9 Hackescher Markt, or
S-Bahn / U-Bahn Friedrichstrasse

To find out more

The Bode Museum also holds Hans Thomann, "The Holy Kinship," ca. 1515 (pictured; in room 215), and "Anna Selbdritt," Vogtland, ca. 1520 (in room 107).

Hans Thomann, "The Holy Kinship," ca. 1515

Cyanide

emotions

The doctor and author Friedrich Wolf (1888–1953) had a sure sense of his topic's explosive nature when he picked the title for his play attacking Sec. 218, Germany's anti-abortion law. The play was called *Cyanide*. When the movie of the same name premiered in 1930 in the Babylon Cinema, Wolf was immediately arrested and the film was banned.

Section 218 remained explosive. When women don't control access to safe contraception, abortion was and remains a social and health problem—often with fatal consequences. Faced with paternalism, hypocrisy, and double standards, women's anger over abortion broke open the route to a new women's movement. Following journalist Alice Schwarzer's call in 1971, celebrities including actress Romy Schneider and hundreds of other women proclaimed, on the cover of the popular news magazine *Stern*: "We had abortions." The scandal was enormous. Section 218 was liberalized, challenged, tightened, and debated, debated, debated. While the West German women's movement was still fighting, in East Germany women achieved the right to abortion on demand in the first trimester as early as 1972. But German unification put an end to that liberal legislation, and unified Germany still grants only very limited options for terminating pregnancy. For religious representatives of all stripes, nothing seems to be as aggravating as women's right to make their own choices about reproduction. Yet all the studies show that the best way to avoid abortions is to give women an unrestricted right to abortion—the best way to help a woman decide to bear a child is to work for socially accepted, financially unproblematic, and medically first-class terminations, embedded in a culture of equal rights that also covers sexuality and contraception.

Location
Babylon cinema,
Rosa-Luxemburg-Strasse 30,
10119 Berlin

How to get there
U 2 Rosa-Luxemburg-Platz

Sources
Criminal Code of the Federal Republic of Germany

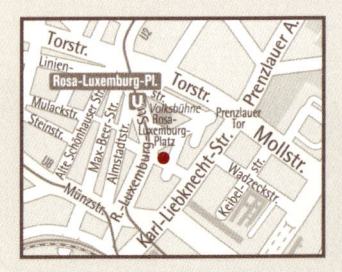

Law on Abortion, March 9, 1972 (German Democratic Republic)

To find out more
Karen Hagemann (ed.), *Eine Frauensache. Alltagsleben und Geburtenpolitik 1919–1933. Eine Ausstellungsdokumentation*, Pfaffenweiler: Centaurus, 1991

No outrage over deaths from unwanted pregnancies and illegal abortions—only over the right to choose

Dime-novel dreams

emotions

The pragmatic view is "If you can't do without it, learn to love it." That may not suit the German penchant for unflinching realism, but Germany hasn't been immune to the idea's charm. It made Hedwig Courths-Mahler (1867–1950) the queen of the German dime novel, with her never-ending string of novels about the never-ending happiness found by poor but golden-hearted women. Hedwig Courths-Mahler is a byword for feel-good women's novels; what Hollywood is for the movie industry, HCM is for the colorful paperback market. She even proudly claimed to have invented the happy ending, and her royalties must be a dream factory all their own. HCM reached these heights through hard work. Her mother was a day laborer, and Hedwig went to school for only four years, yet she grasped the era's taste for passion and melodrama with both bravura and precision. Even today, professors reach for her books to illustrate their lectures on social history. In HCM's stories, every flaw in women's realities is healed with the same relentless prescription: social mobility achieved through a stubborn struggle for love.

With so much light, shadows can't be far away. The envious made cruel puns on her unusual name, and while male kitsch from Karl May to Ernst Jünger was venerated by respectable clubs, HCM never made it into the bourgeois bookcase—though she certainly ruled the kitchen shelf and nightstand.

The Nazis demanded HCM stories set among the SS, their villains drawn with Jewish features; the author refused to comply. Postwar West Germany rejected her applications for rationed paper. East Germany banned her works: women's destiny was now to be improved in real life, not fantasy. Yet Hedwig Courths-Mahler is still read. As they say, if you can't do without it, you might as well embrace it ...

Location
Commemorative plaque at Dönhoffstrasse 11, 10318 Berlin

How to get there
S 3 Karlshorst

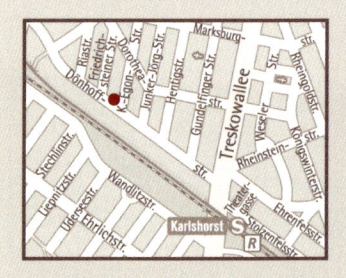

Source
Regina Söffker and Jutta Wolf, *Lust auf Lichtenberg*, Berlin: Neunplus1 Verlag, 2004

To find out more
www.dhm.de/lemo/html/
   biografien/CourthsMahlerHedwig
Excerpt (in German) at
   www.bastei.de/beitrag/
   standardbeitrag_17386.html

Dreaming in Karlshorst

Dogs

emotions

Location
All over Berlin

He's everywhere. He is loved and cherished. His desire for freedom is given full rein; so is his need for affection. He knows no class distinctions, no national borders, no prejudice. He brings together young and old, rich and poor, rascal and epicure. He's a dog.

The dog is avant-garde. His role as a paragon of obedience is passé–nowadays he has a greater task to fulfill, as a hero on the road into the future. He can do what no one else can: overcome the boundary between the animal and the human world. His universe is the universe of his master or mistress. He shares bed, couch, and bowl with them, joy, pain, and din-dins with them. He knows their irritation, their step, their laugh. He's their mirror. Together they are a unit, permanent and inseparable, till death do them part.

People are becoming more and more isolated; he walks among them. People are becoming more and more lonely; he gives them company. There's no park bench he won't sprawl on, no lawn he won't romp on, no sidewalk he doesn't decorate with the evidence of his excellent lunch, no crowded train he doesn't demand to squeeze into. Where children are a noisy nuisance, he's a king–king by the grace of master and mistress. You'd better not forget to raise your hat. You'd better not ask where his leash is. You'd better show that your heart overflows when he wags his tail. There must be no space between dog and soul.

The law applies to everybody; not to him. He is freedom and anarchy. He is love and never-disappointed trust. He is the extension of our ego into the world and into the gutter. He shows the world what we think of it. He gives us something to hold onto in a world that keeps turning its face away. He is us, and therefore he is good. A dog's life: something that women can only dream of.

A sense of the pack in the big city's anonymity

Facts of life

emotions

In her memoirs, the physician and health campaigner Käte Frankenthal (1889–1976) wrote: "I matched every category that was abhorred by the Nazis: Jew, socialist, political representative, emancipated woman …. There was nothing left for me in Germany …."

Frankenthal, who came from a Jewish family, was one of the first women to achieve a license to practice medicine in Germany, qualifying in 1914. As a district councilor, a member of the city council assembly, and the municipal physician for the district of Neukölln, she took a vehement stand in favor of contraception and sex education, and against the ban on abortion (➤ **Cyanide**). The more she saw of the city's social and health problems, the more important political activism became—especially as she was the only woman on the budget, health, and welfare committees. It was thanks to Käte Frankenthal's commitment that Berlin's municipal sexual counseling offices handed out free contraception in the late 1920s. She was also the driving force behind a 1930 decree by the municipality that women's family planning should be supported by providing counseling and birth control at no cost. In her own practice, which she ran until 1928 while working as a medical resident at the prestigious Charité Hospital, she counseled women and girls on sex and marriage, distributed free contraceptives, and also helped her patients—most of them very poor—to find housing, food, and clothing. When the Nazis came to power, Käte Frankenthal was forced to emigrate. The new guidelines on population policy were euthanasia and forced sterilization on the one hand, motherhood medals and Aryan breeding programs on the other. The needs and hardships of women were irrelevant.

Location
FFGZ (Feminist Women's Health Center), Bamberger Strasse 51, 10777 Berlin

How to get there
U 3, 9 Spichernstrasse,
U 4 Viktoria-Luise-Platz

Sources
Bernhard Meyer, *Eine Medizinerin in der Politik*, Berlin: Edition Luisenstadt, 1999

www.luise-berlin.de
www.berlin.de/sen/frauen/oeff-raum/
    plakataktion
Claudia von Gélieu and Bezirksamt Neu-
    kölln (eds), *Das Frauenviertel Rudow*,
    Berlin: Bezirksamt Neukölln, 2003

To find out more
Käte Frankenthal, *Der dreifache Fluch:
    Jüdin, Intellektuelle, Sozialistin. Lebens-
    erinnerungen einer Ärztin in Deutsch-
    land und im Exil*, Frankfurt: Campus
    Verlag, 1981

Women-friendly medical care still can't be taken for granted.

Honor

emotions

In February 2005, the young Berliner Hatun Sürücü was murdered by her brother (→ Not my bag). Her family had been unable to tolerate the fact that Hatun had freed herself from a forced marriage and built up her own independent life with her son, complete with an apartment, vocational training, and her own choice of partner. The code of honor—control over the female members of the family—had been violated, and a dead sister was better than that.

While the talk shows, newspaper supplements, and integration-policy summits discussed Islam-influenced parallel universes in sometimes horrified, sometimes conciliatory tones, some young Muslim men praised the act of violence for the TV cameras, all in the name of honor. The murder had brought to light a widespread rejection of the western way of life: "Don't be like the Germans!" That refers not to western social or technological achievements, which are happily adopted, but essentially gender roles, equal rights, and self-determination—the core of a democratic vision of the human being (→ Multiculti).

A closer look reveals that many boys and girls are trying to escape this populist, fundamentalist way of thinking and acting. They are open to democratic values and want to enjoy western freedoms, often without knowing how they can achieve that under the strict supervision of their own community.

The girls in Neukölln's MaDonna girls' club wanted to do something to oppose oppression and murder. They were joined by boys who wanted to free themselves from the violent role they were being forced to take as their sisters' minders. The result was a postcard campaign with the motto "Honor = fighting for my sister's freedom." Courageous girls and boys were standing up for liberty and equal rights.

Location
MaDonna Mädchenkult.Ur e.V.,
Falkstrasse 26, 12053 Berlin

How to get there
U 8 Boddinstrasse

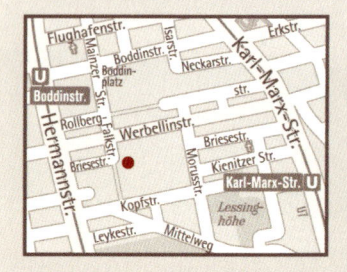

Source

Gabriele Heinemann, "Mädchentreff oder Hurenclub? Soziale Ausgrenzung und Fundamentalismus sind Herausforderungen für die Jugendhilfe," *unsere jugend* 3/2006

To find out more
www.frauenrechte.de
www.zwangsheirat.de

Muslim girls want the same rights as their brothers and as other girls.

Ideal

emotions

When we talk about the ideal, beauty is never far away. Beauty—women's secret weapon and their Achilles' heel. Beauty is in the eye of the beholder, and changes constantly: tough luck for those who do their best to conform, and tough luck for those who don't. Beauty is the knockout argument against every woman, an argument that just refuses to die.

The proof that beauty is relative can be found in the plump goddess of prehistoric times, the Baroque's love of earthiness, the balancing act between decency and décolleté, the starvation artist Twiggy—the view changes over the years, but its object is always woman. It's an unforgiving gaze, taught by the media and cast millions upon millions of times. Especially by women.

The trade shows of beauty demand victims. Thinner and thinner, half-starved, bearing emblems of prostitution, violence, and rape, women tread the catwalk as high priestesses of the beauty ideal. Their bodies are mined for cultural capital and economic profit. All over the world, girls dream of taking their place: a model, not a woman. Women are more than willing to carry out the necessary adjustments themselves, paying a high price in money, pain, vitality, and life expectancy. No dictatorship has seemed so gentle as the dictate of beauty, yet its implacability can compete with the worst of them. Hungry or shivering with cold, their feet bound or their waists pinched, caged and exhibited, cut open, cut down, puffed up, anaesthetized, bleached, cauterized—the aids and appliances of women's beauty would not be out of place in a chamber of horrors, and no police intervention is required.

Some clever woman wrote on the remnants of the now superfluous Berlin Wall: "All women are beautiful, everywhere." Now that's a beautiful ideal.

Location
"The Earth,"
by Ingeborg Hunzinger,
Monbijou Park, 10117 Berlin

How to get there
S 5, 7, 9 Hackescher Markt,
S 1, 2 Oranienburger Strasse

Source
Familienplanungszentrum Balance e. V., Mauritiuskirchstrasse 3, 10365 Berlin: "Erklärung zum Internationalen Frauentag 2008"

If you want to be beautiful, you can't afford to give a hoot about ideals.

Knut

emotions

He's so cute! That is, he *was* so cute. Polar bear baby Knut, rejected by his mother and brought up by an affectionate zookeeper, became an international sensation. The world saw a man who spent day and night caring for the helpless little creature, feeding it with a bottle, stroking it, warming it, and heroically coping with sleep deprivation. Under his protection, the little cub thrived and the zookeeper could play with him, comfort him, teach him, and build up a relationship that everyone, experts and zoo-goers alike, could see was deep and strong.

Women all over the world watched, enchanted. What a model father that man was! No trace there of an evolutionary incapacity for parenting, not a hint of masculinity being lost through love and patience, and not even a decline in attractiveness to the opposite sex. Myths came tumbling down. The hunter and gatherer is, it turns out, in fact quite capable of active fatherhood—as proved by a little bear. Imagine having a father like Knut's! All the story seemed to lack was a wife for Knut. Let's hope that the myth-busting miracle of his upbringing continues and that more surprises are to come. That would be nice for baby bears and good fathers, happy mothers, and a future where men can relate to women in other ways than just needing them for one purpose or another.

Location
Berlin Zoo, Hardenbergplatz 8, 10787 Berlin
Knut died suddenly on March 19, 2011.

How to get there
S-Bahn/U-Bahn Zoologischer Garten

To find out more
www.zoo-berlin.de/zoo.html

A little bear with a big impact

Nuns

emotions

For Catholics, Berlin is a kind of diaspora, yet the convent Regina Martyrum Carmel is a phenomenon that typifies today's multireligious, often atheist, Berlin. It's typical because the nuns, like many other religious communities, attend to the concerns of the city. It's also typical because the diversity of religions results in both tolerance and obstinacy—and the nuns of the Carmelite convent are both tolerant and obstinate in a very special way.

The convent was built in 1983, an offshoot of the Carmelite convent of the Precious Blood that is located on the grounds of the Dachau concentration camp. Since then, the eleven Carmelite nuns have been managing the Plötzensee Prison memorial. Between 1933 and 1945, the Nazis beheaded, hanged, or strangled 2,891 people in this prison, including the conspirators in the July 20, 1944, attempt to assassinate Hitler.

The nuns keep alive the memory of the Nazi dictatorship's victims. But they also pray for very modern things—for young people who don't know where to turn, for single parents, and always for a peaceful world. The nearby Maria Regina Martyrum memorial church has room for everybody: Jewish, Christian, Muslim, Buddhist, and atheist women and men seek tranquility and counsel with the nuns. Tending memorials is always an ecumenical activity; as the sisters say, it was not only Catholics who were executed at Plötzensee. Once a year, the nuns extend a special invitation to young women to spend a day at the convent, and there are also retreats and meditation days. Naturally, there's also a cloister shop selling good things from the gardens, kitchens, and workshops of cloisters around the country. When it comes to shopping, at least, Berlin traditionally calls out for dedicated missionaries.

Location
Convent and convent shop,
Heckerdamm 232, 13627 Berlin

How to get there
U 7 Jakob-Kaiser-Platz,
Bus 123 Friedrich-Olbricht-Damm/
Heckerdamm

Sources

www.karmel-berlin.de
www.luise-berlin.de
die tageszeitung, May 26, 27, and 28, 2007

The end of a hard day's work: Carmelite nun walking home

Pleasure

emotions

Pleasure is at home in Berlin. What's your own pleasure: strolling in the 17th-century Lustgarten or visiting one of the city's summer residences, dedicated to leisure? Sipping epicurean cocktails, dancing the night away, or, best of all, going shopping in one of Berlin's innumerable malls? Perhaps even a visit to the Beate Uhse Erotic Museum, despite justified doubts that it will contain any objects dedicated to female lust?

La Luna, the women's sex shop, is a different matter. Based in the WeiberWirtschaft complex (→ Business by and for women), it was one of the first of its kind. But why the hurry? Isn't female pleasure an endless deferral? And, of course, also a mystery: What do women want? The question kept Sigmund Freud busy for a whole lifetime of research. And what did he discover? Nothing but his own view of the world: penis envy. Oh well!

Nowadays women have provided a few answers of their own, things that Freud himself could have heard from his female patients if he'd been a little bit braver. The sensational reports by the Kinseys and Shere Hite initiated a journey into the labyrinth of feminine lust. At its focus was the renaissance of the center of female pleasure, a small but important organ that had lost some of its public reputation through the fame of the phallus. Above all, though, women began to talk about their lust and their dreams, outside the sphere of science. The time had come to rediscover the fact that pleasure begins in the mind and in the practical circumstances of life. In Berlin, publisher Gudula Lorez (1944–1987) (→ Second Life) asked for women to send in their erotic writings, and the response was huge. Taking our own desires seriously and combating misogynist pornography—those are the major concerns of lusty feminists even today.

Location
Floating restaurant Alte Liebe ("Old Love"), Havelchaussee 107 at Am Postfenn, 14055 Berlin

How to get there
S 75, 9 Pichelsberg,
Bus 218 Am Postfenn

Sources
Christiane Olivier, *Jokastes Kinder. Die Psyche der Frau im Schatten der Mutter*, Munich: Econ, 1989

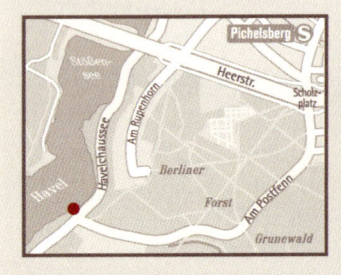

Alice Schwarzer, *Der kleine Unterschied und seine großen Folgen*, Frankfurt: Fischer, 1990

To find out more
Gudula Lorez, Sandgeflüster. *Erotische Reisegeschichten: Frauen gehen fremd*, Munich: Gudula Lorez, 1989
Gudula Lorez (ed.), *Wo die Nacht den Tag umarmt. Erotische Phantasien und Geschichten von Frauen*, Reinbek: Rowohlt, 1992
www.laluna-toys.de

"Old Love" and pleasure meet on the lake

Queer

emotions

They danced through the lavender nights of the 1920s (→ Twinkle toes), reading *Girlfriend* magazine and sauntering as stylish femmes and butches along the streets of the pulsing metropolis. Forced to hide from the Nazi regime and its ideal of Germanic womanhood, they were sometimes persecuted, sometimes ignored. They spent the narrow-minded years of postwar reconstruction in the closet, shielding their love from the public gaze and developing a small but well-formed universe of lesbian life in the "sub," the subculture of women's bars and clubs. With the advent of the women's movement, they finally came out: in the Berlin Lesbian Action Center, at exhilarating women's parties dancing to the Flying Lesbians, and on marches, provoking bystanders with energy and relish.

Although Berlin was never just a shining El Dorado for lesbians, it was certainly easier to live and love here than in other cities, let alone in the provinces. Even today, young lesbians and gay men continue to make their way unerringly to Berlin.

With East Berlin's Sunday Club and sometimes under the protection of the church, East Germany, too, took cautious steps toward emancipation.

Society is getting used to seeing openly lesbian and gay people in politics and public office. Lesbians are saying "I do" at the registry office; lesbian mothers are getting involved in kindergartens, schools, and youth services; it's no longer rare to have a lesbian neighbor, colleague, fellow student, or sports teammate. Hostility and discrimination, silence and denigration still exist, but less and less. And Berlin's government pursues anti-discrimination policies that also give support to lesbians, gay men, and other queer Berliners.

Location
RuT – Rad und Tat e.V.,
Schillerpromenade 1,
12049 Berlin

How to get there
U 8 Boddinstrasse

To find out more
www.lilaarchiv.de
Equal opportunities office:
Landesstelle für Gleichbehand-
 lung – gegen Diskriminierung,
www.berlin.de/lb/ads/
www.lesbischeinitiativerut.de
www.berlin-judentum.de/
 denkmal/rosenstrasse-1.htm

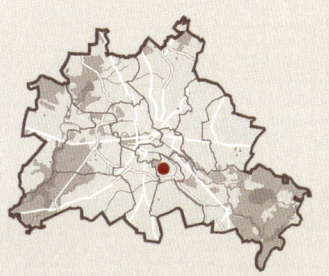

Different from the others?

Rose

emotions

Just a few steps away from Alexanderplatz, tucked away on Rosenstrasse, is a little square containing large red sandstone sculptures tinted with green moss. It was here that something astounding happened in the Nazi era: open resistance to the regime and to the abduction of Jews. The protagonists in this drama were women, despite the masculinity cult of the day, which celebrated men as warrior heroes and women as (at most) the heroines of childbirth, and despite the culture of memorializing anti-Nazi resistance, which usually reduces women to the role of couriers. On Rosenstrasse it was women who truly showed courage, who stood up for their beliefs, who defied the police and the SS and their own fear on the open street, and who won the battle: they had their Jewish husbands and children released.

During the "Factory Action" of February 1943, thousands of Jewish men and youths were arrested at their workplaces, and those who were the husbands or children of non-Jewish women were brought here to Rosenstrasse. Their wives and mothers, supported by friends, protested noisily, gathering hundreds at a time in front of the building and refusing to be intimidated even by the threats of the SS. After six days, the command to release the men arrived.

What happened to the Jewish wives and children of non-Jewish men? Nothing is known about that. The memorial to the heroines of Rosenstrasse, the work of sculptor Ingeborg Hunzinger, was not erected until fifty years after the protests. It also memorializes the Old Synagogue of 1714, the Jewish ritual bathhouse, and the Jewish social welfare office, which were all located here before the Holocaust.

Location
Memorials, Rosenstrasse, 10178 Berlin

How to get there
Tram M 4, M 5, M 6, Bus 100, 200
Spandauer Strasse

Source
www.berlin-judentum.de/denkmal/rosenstrasse-1.htm

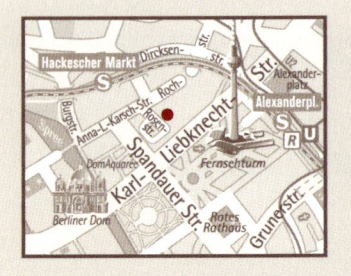

To find out more

Gernot Jochheim, *Frauenprotest in der Rosenstraße Berlin 1943*, Berlin: Hentrich & Hentrich, 1990

Nathan Stoltzfus, *Widerstand des Herzens. Der Aufstand der Berliner Frauen in der Rosenstraße – 1943*, Munich: dtv, 2002

Rosenstrasse, dir. Margarethe von Trotta, Germany 2003

Women stood up here to claim victory over death.

Softly, Peterkin, softly ...

emotions

A young woman sits in a summer garden; three small children play peacefully on the flower-studded lawn, accompanying their game with rhymes, maybe "Little Rabbit in the Hollow" or "Rumpumpel's Dancing." Later, the golden crickets chirp, the moon has risen over the house, she sings the children to sleep: "Softly, Peterkin, softly ...."

The young woman is Paula Dehmel, who wrote her children nursery rhymes, stories, and songs that were full of vivacity, colloquialism, and poetry. Even today, her lines still form an indispensable part of the repertoire of German kindergartens, although the idyll in which they were written now seems like a fairy tale itself.

Paula was born in 1862 as the daughter of Julius Oppenheimer, rabbi of the Jewish reform congregation on Johannisstrasse. She enjoyed her childhood in an open-minded family. She and her siblings would gather to listen to the stories their father told so skillfully, and Paula carried on the tradition. She learned to read early, reciting poems with enthusiasm. The empathetic atmosphere of Paula's childhood in the heyday of assimilated, liberal German Jewish life, her great musical and literary talent, and not least the support and encouragement of her husband Richard all flowed into her work. In 1895 the Dehmels published their first children's book; their breakthrough came with *Fitzebutze* (1900) and *Rumpumpel* (1903).

A successful author, a wonderful hostess, and a patron of young artists, Paula Dehmel lived in Pankow and Wilhelmsaue until 1918. At the end of World War I, the world of her childhood lay in ruins—but her poetry still enchants both parents and children today.

Location
Commemorative plaque at Parkstrasse 56, 13187 Berlin

How to get there
Tram 50, Bus 250, 255 Rathaus Pankow

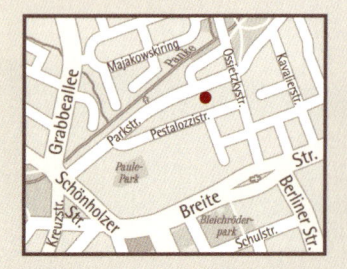

Source

Ulla Jung, "Ich möchte euch alle miteinander…," in *SpurenSuche. Frauen in Pankow*, Berlin: Bezirksamt Pankow von Berlin, 2002

To find out more

Paula Dehmel, *Rumpumpel*, Berlin: Agora Verlag, 1987

"Leise, Peterle, leise, der Mond geht auf die Reise…"

In diesem Haus lebte von 1893 bis 1899 die Kinderbuchautorin

Paula Dehmel
31.12.1862 – 8.7.1918

zusammen mit ihrem Mann, dem Lyriker Richard Dehmel, und ihren drei Kindern. Mit Gedichten und Märchen von Paula Dehmel sind Generationen von Kindern aufgewachsen.

The children's poet and her cozy nest

Twinkle toes

emotions

Pas de deux or dirty dancing, ballroom or techno: a dedicated website announces every day's parties and events, dance workshops and festivals in Berlin. Dance partner exchanges offer partners for the waltz, fox-trot, or cha-cha. Berliners dance in ballrooms, dance schools, cafés, and clubs, but they can also be found in the Volksbühne theater's Green Salon, in the pavilion at Friedrichshain park, or in summertime under the Museum Island colonnade in front of the New Museum.

In Berlin, dancing has always been popular entertainment, cheap and fun: the current mayor's description of the city as "poor but sexy" has a very long tradition. In Kaiser Wilhelm's days, cooks, maids, and nannies went to the hop, wearing out their shoes with polkas and polonaises. If they were lucky, there were no consequences(➤ Cyanide). In the 1920s, higher society took to the floor for a Charleston. The ladies' world in Berlin had a head start even then (➤ Queer).

After the war—bombed out, traumatized, struggling with debt, and trying to survive on skimpy rations—Berliners danced into an uncertain future with astonishing verve. The new sound, with its boogie-woogie, jitterbug, and swing, fanned their enthusiasm for America and Americans. It helped them forget the misery of the Third Reich and its ruins.

Love Parade and techno raves, the tango wave and the ballroom boom, crazy clubs and Café Keese's table telephones—when it comes to dancing, every generation invents its very own culture of flirtation. One thing does unite the different dance scenes: the reserved attitude of men in couple dances. But in a city as queer as Berlin, that's no problem. Here, same-sex dancing has reached sophisticated heights, no matter what team you play for.

Location
TangoArt, Alte Bahnhofshalle
Friedenau, Bahnhofstrasse 4d,
12159 Berlin

How to get there
S 1 Friedenau

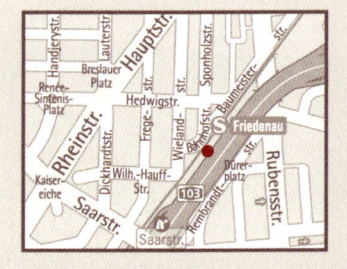

Source
Daniel Haaksman, "Verschwende deine Jugend," *Spiegel online*, July 14, 2007

To find out more
www.tangoart.de
www.tanzeninberlin.de
www.pinkballroom.de
Dancing with Myself, film documentary by Antje Kruska and Judith Keil, Berlin Film Festival 2005

Life's passion—tango and other pleasantries

atmospheres

BiOriental
märchenhaft einkaufen
Maybachufer
Wochenmarkt
Die + Fr
11-18:30 Uhr
markt

Almancilar

atmospheres

Almancilar is a Turkish word meaning something like "Germany-ers." It's the name given in Turkey to the many Turkish women and men who have been living and working in Berlin and other parts of Germany since the 1960s. Today it would be impossible to imagine many of Berlin's districts without Turkish people, stores, and institutions. Two countries, two languages, two cultures—enrichment and challenge at once. The challenges, especially for women, are highly publicized, with buzzwords like head-covering, forced marriage, or honor killing. Turkish women, like women everywhere, have to fight to achieve self-determination and a life without violence (→ **Honor,** → Multiculti).

But beyond these difficult debates, there is also a relaxed and enjoyable coexistence. The colorful market along the Landwehr Canal at Maybachufer is part of that. Women with headscarves and without pick their way through the long series of stalls that line the canalside street. Market women raise their voices to attract attention, mountains of fruit and vegetables change hands—and as a kind concession to the single-person household, the traders will also sell small quantities. The whole scene is marked by a mix of dynamism and serenity; everyone here wants to take their time. It only remains to mention the tea seller, maneuvering his way through the crowds with a tray of tea glasses.

Location
Maybachufer market, Tuesdays and Fridays, 12 noon to 6:30 p.m., Maybachufer, 12047 Berlin

How to get there
U 8 Schönleinstrasse

A moment's respite from the tensions of integration policy

Big mouth, big heart

atmospheres

Ick sitze da und esse Klops.
Uff eenmal kloppt's.
Ick sitze, kieke, wundre mir,
uff eenmal is se uff die Tür.
Nanu denk ick, ick denk nanu!
Jetzt is se uff, erst war se zu.
Ick jehe raus und kieke,
und wer steht draußen? Icke.

In this well-known poem in Berlin dialect, the narrator looks up from a dish of meatballs to answer a knock at the door. The door is mysteriously open, the poet goes out to investigate, and "Who do I find outside? Me." The city's dialect is famous for its laconic, brusque, and working-class humor, with a tendency to go straight for the jugular and a refusal to respect authority in any shape or form. Mockery and self-mockery are its bread and butter.

When the wit, poetry, and philosophy of the street combine at a high level of reflexivity, seasoned with self-deprecation and amazing understatement—or, occasionally, shameless showing off—there's only one possible culprit: it has to be a "Berlin flower," whether her roots are Pomeranian, Silesian, Westphalian, Berlin, Italian, Turkish, or Russian (➤ **Berlin flower**, ➤ **Mount Rubble**).

Keep your ears open!

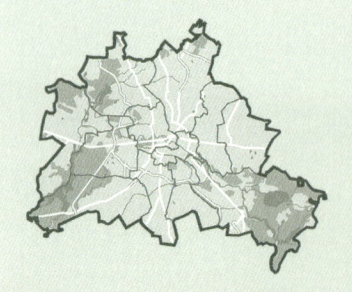

A sassy Berlin poet at work on the S-Bahn arches, Mitte district

Birthing center

atmospheres

In 1987, five midwives established Germany's first birthing center, at Klausenerplatz in the heart of Charlottenburg. All of them were employed in Berlin clinics, and all shared a critical view of the conditions for new mothers in that era: coldly functional labor rooms, overuse of painkillers, midwives changing shifts during a labor, and newborns taken away for examination immediately after birth. At a time when carefully scheduled birth was at the top of the doctors' wish list, the birthing center movement heralded a radical change of course. The basic idea was that, in general, a woman can give birth to her child herself; she doesn't have to have it "delivered." And, most importantly, women don't want to give birth in an atmosphere that leaves them clinically clean, sterile, and disenfranchised.

Based on the World Health Organization criteria, around 70 percent of all births in Germany can be classified as normal births that require no medical intervention. Yet not even 10 percent of these low-risk births in fact do without medical interference. Almost 29 percent of births in Germany are carried out by Caesarean section!

With their slogan "Childbirth is not a disease," the birthing center movement, as part of the women's movement, successfully put childbirth into a different light and changed the day-to-day realities on mainstream maternity wards as well. Nowadays, the priority is no longer the smoothest possible operation of the clinic, but the well-being of mother and child. In the birthing centers, midwives see their role as dependable guides during pregnancy, at the birth itself, and in the months that follow. However, in terms of natural childbirth Germany is still a backward nation, with a home-birth rate of only around 2 percent (→ Expecting).

Location
Geburtshaus Charlottenburg,
Spandauer Damm 130,
14050 Berlin

How to get there
S 41, 42 Westend,
Bus M 45 Klausenerplatz

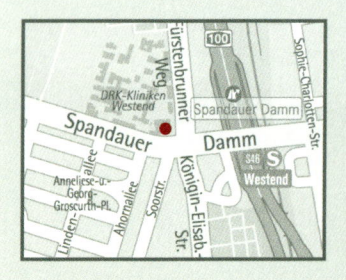

Source
www.geburtshaus-berlin.de

To find out more
www.hebammenforschung.de

Almost like home—keeping childbirth local

Fisimatenten

atmospheres

Berliners prefer apartments on the *beletage*, or second floor; now and again they find themselves in a *bredouille*, or in trouble; they fry a mean *bulette*, or burger; and are none too pleased when someone causes *fisimatenten*.

Berlin's vocabulary is full of French words, many of which are no longer visible as such. *Kinkerlitzchen* (knickknacks), for example, comes from *quincaillerie*, *ratzekahl* from *radical*, *mausetot* ("dead as a mouse") *from mort si tôt*, and so on (→ Boulette and mocca faux).

No other European metropolis shows such deep-rooted French influence as Berlin. The evidence is there in Franco-Berlin couples such as Voltaire and Friedrich II or Marlene Dietrich and Jean Gabin.

In the late 17th century, the Great Elector gave sanctuary to Huguenots fleeing persecution in France. French was spoken at court and in higher social circles, so Huguenot governesses were highly sought after, teaching language, etiquette, and table manners. That was *temps perdu*, judging by the manners of present-day Berliners, but it was ladies of French heritage who perfected the salon culture of 18th- and 19th-century Berlin (→ Salon).

Nowadays, the new Berlin, cheap to get to and still so raw and mutable, is drawing young French people who appreciate the lively, comparatively inexpensive city with its unbuilt space and new opportunities. Nonprofit organizations, schools and research centers, museums, theaters and cinemas, corporations, stores and restaurants all bear witness to a renewed Franco-German alliance. By the way, *Visitez ma tente* (visit my tent) is what Napoleon's occupying soldiers are supposed to have called out to the pert girls of Berlin. Worried mothers warned their enterprising daughters "not to get up to any *fisimatenten*."

Location
French Cathedral with Huguenot Museum, Gendarmenmarkt, 10117 Berlin

How to get there
U 2 Stadtmitte

Sources

Cyril Buffet, *Fisimatenten. Franzosen in Berlin und Brandenburg*, Berlin: Ausländerbeauftragte des Berliner Senats, 1997

Conrad Grau, "Berlin, Französische Straße. Auf den Spuren der Hugenotten," *Illustrierte Historische Hefte* 46, East Berlin: Deutscher Verlag der Wissenschaften, 1987

For rent

atmospheres

In Berlin you can certainly rent more than just apartments, cars, bicycles, or lawn chairs. Clever cosmopolitans in the capital don't buy Gucci, Prada, or Dior bags, they rent them. It costs only a fraction of the true price, but for those who value that kind of thing when going out, it makes the same impression.

Speaking of going out: There are also options for women who don't want to go out alone, to the theater, for example, or to explore the city. Special agencies refer actors, architects, artists, or athletes to accompany you dancing or sailing or to play tennis. And anyone who prefers to explore Berlin with a woman should contact Laura Méritt. She runs Europe's only escort service by and for women.

Since everyone knows that Berliners are outspoken for all kinds of causes, to satisfy a totally different rental need hired protesters are at your service. No matter what you support or oppose, you can rent committed personnel to hit the streets with your desired slogans. And for the Berlinale film festival it is possible for cineastes pressed for time to rent students to stand in line to buy tickets (→ Lola).

Berlin is a city of renters—even down to the details.

Location
Mimi – Textile Antiquitäten (vintage clothing rental), Goltzstrasse 5, 10781 Berlin

How to get there
U 7 Eisenacher Strasse

Source
akzente 4/2007

It's all a matter of the presentation.

Green thumbs

atmospheres

It's hard to believe: There are more than thirty agricultural businesses in Berlin. That isn't really surprising since the city used to be many separate villages, from which it grew to its present size. Also, Berlin itself was for a long time active in agriculture. In 1922 the Berliner Stadtgüter (municipal farms) company was founded; at the time it cultivated almost 62,000 acres (25,000 ha.) of land. Summer 2007 marked the end of this episode of urban influence on the rural economy, since the last of Berlin's municipal farms was privatized. The present agricultural businesses in Berlin, many of which have been passed down from one generation to the next, can hardly still be considered farms in a classical sense. Horses and rental stable space often secure the livelihood of the owners.

"Every farm needs the strength of a woman," announced the president of Berlin's Association of Rural Women in her kitchen in Lübars, in northern Berlin, where lunch is always served at exactly 12 noon. The association represents and promotes the interests of rural women in Berlin. Their goals include networking and offering specialized training and continuing education for women. The village of Lübars, with its well-maintained structure and an idyllic panorama of Märkisches Viertel, a large-scale housing project, offers insight into the rural Berlin of the past.

There are many places in the city where women can breathe in good country air, such as Domäne Dahlem, a Berlin farm that can be reached by subway. This agricultural business is only half an hour from Kurfürstendamm and is an agrarian historical open-air museum with cultivated fields and animal husbandry. Here women can browse in the farm store and drink coffee under the trees. But that's not all—tractor tours are also offered.

Location
Alt-Lübars, 13469 Berlin

How to get there
Bus 222 Alt-Lübars (end of the line)

Sources
Berliner Landfrauenverband e.V., women's section of the Landesverband Gartenbau und Landwirtschaft Berlin-Brandenburg e.V.

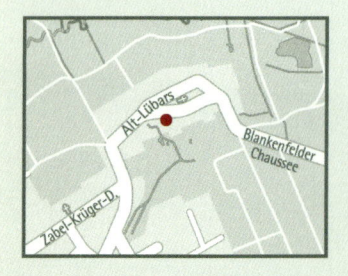

www.domaene-dahlem.de
www.grueneliga-berlin.de

To find out more
Berliner Landfrauenverband e.V.,
  contact: Frau Kühne-Sironski,
  president, Alt-Lübars 27,
  13469 Berlin, Tel: (030) 4 02 53 95

Berliners can do anything: even "village."

Humboldt

atmospheres

Most people have heard of the brothers Wilhelm and Alexander von Humboldt, who left such a lasting mark on the history of German science and humanities. But would these men's achievements really have been possible without the influence and intervention of their family's women (➤ Clio)? In a letter to a female friend, Wilhelm von Humboldt wrote of his future wife Caroline: "… to hear her, see her, live with her will give my principles more constancy, my mind higher perspectives, my action more efficacy and force, my heart more serenity.…"

The Humboldt women's unusual level of education, their open-mindedness and joie de vivre had an inspiring effect on Berlin society. The circle of their friends included great names of the period such as Queen Luise of Prussia (➤ Queens), Johann Wolfgang von Goethe, Friedrich and Charlotte von Schiller, Caroline von Wolzogen, Angelica Kauffman, Christian Daniel Rauch, and Friedrich Wilhelm von Schadow (➤ Salon). The biographies of Marie Elisabeth, Caroline, Adelheid, Gabriele, and Constanze von Humboldt also mark a period of European upheaval, from 1741 to 1920. They show the Humboldt women not only as multilingual cosmopolitans, as salonières and artists, highly educated in science and religion, but also as wives, mothers, and householders—these were women moving between tradition and radical new beginnings. Caroline and Wilhelm von Humboldt lived in Tegel Palace, extending it on designs by Schinkel. The palace and its wonderful gardens were the Humboldt family's home and favorite spot. It's also where they built their mausoleum. In the surrounding district of Reinickendorf many places (the docks, library, and more) are named after Wilhelm, but why not commemorate Caroline or Adelheid as well?

Location
Tegel Palace (open for viewing in summer), Gabrielenstrasse/Adelheidallee 19, 13507 Berlin

How to get there
U 6 Alt-Tegel,
Bus 133, 222 An der Mühle

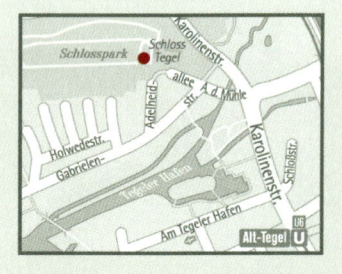

Sources

Flyer for the exhibition "Die Frauen der Familie von Humboldt," Heimatmuseum Reinickendorf, March 2006

Beate Neubauer, *Schönheit, Grazie und Geist. Die Frauen der Familie von Humboldt*, Berlin: Edition Ebersbach, 2007

Caroline's farsightedness is still inspiring today.

Lisa and Jackie

atmospheres

The girls' club named "LiSA" was born in 1982 in the neighborhood around Klausenerplatz. LiSA has roamed around a bit since then, and can now be found in a villa behind the noisy Spandauer Damm. She's the brainchild of migrant women who came to Berlin as "guest workers," got involved in the women's movement, and wanted to create leisure spaces for their daughters outside the family. Like her sisters Mädchenladen Wedding, MaDonna in Neukölln (➤ Honor), and Café Pink in Schöneberg, LiSA too believes that migrant and other women of color can't simply be absorbed into the feminism of their white sisters, that they need a voice and articulation of their own.

LiSA is generous and combative, always cash-strapped, sassy, and inventive. She invites girls from every country in the world to test their strength as the whim takes them, to be angry (and take advantage of a free anger-training program), cheerful, ambitious, or sad. LiSA encourages girls to become full human beings, self-willed, independent, open to life and to other people.

LiSA now also has a little sister, the summer sports project Jackie. Jackie likes to be out and about, and if you can't find her at home on Jakob-Kaiser-Platz then she may be in the brightly painted construction trailer nearby. Jackie has absolutely no intention of leaving the streets to the boys. She enjoys running riot through the public space just as much as they do. And her band *Böse Mädchen*, " Bad Girls," helps create the right mood. But despite Jackie's company, LiSA has too few sisters—and far too many brothers who have no truck with girls.

LiSA is now twenty-five, and she thinks it's high time the money available for youth work started being distributed equally between girls and boys.

Location
Jugendzentrum Alte Feuerwache,
Axel-Springer-Strasse 40–41,
10969 Berlin

How to get there
U 2 Spittelmarkt, U 6 Kochstrasse,
Bus M 29 Axel-Springer-Strasse /
Oranienstrasse

To find out more

Interkultureller Mädchen- und Frauenladen LiSA e.V., Spandauer Damm 65 (back building), 14059 Berlin

Can-do women create spaces for can-do girls

Lola

atmospheres

It seems like German cinema began with Marlene Dietrich's naughty Lola in *The Blue Angel*, but it sure hasn't ended with her. Lola has remained loyal to German cinema. Hanna Schygulla played her in 1981 in Fassbinder's film by the same name, and Franka Potente was in remarkable shape when bringing her back to modern cinema in 1998 in Tom Tykwer's ➤ **Run, Lola, Run**. And the Golden Lola–the German film prize–is awarded every year in May in Berlin.

In the meantime the city has itself become a star in the film industry. Attractive as a film location, Berlin serves in many movies and television productions as a backdrop, whether attractive or rundown, hypermodern or historical. Even Hollywood teams with world-class stars such as Jodie Foster and Nicole Kidman shoot in Berlin and Babelsberg.

Women stopped leaving film production up to men a long time ago. The most famous female film producer in Berlin is probably Regina Ziegler, who was even honored in 2006 with a retrospective in New York's Museum of Modern Art. This marked the first time the MoMA commemorated the work of a woman. However, there are also smaller production companies run by women that are attracting attention. The IT WORKS! Media company, founded by Annekatrin Hendel, and Rois Pictures, the new film distribution and production company of actress Sophie Rois, for example, want finally to have a say in deciding what films make it to the movie theaters (➤ **Showtime**).

Berlin is definitely an El Dorado for movie junkies. With eighty-five movie theaters it has the highest cinema density in all of Germany. And each year in February, the Berlinale has no problem increasing the dosage.

Location
Grave of Marlene Dietrich,
Friedhof Stubenrauchstrasse 43,
12161 Berlin

How to get there
U 9, S 41, 42, 47 Bundesplatz

Sources
www.berlin-friedenau.com
www.ziegler-film.com
www.itworksmedien.de
www.roispictures.de

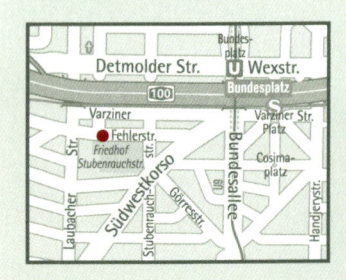

To find out more

Markus Münch, *Drehort Berlin*, berlin edition, 2007

Regina Aggio, *Filmstadt Berlin 1895–2006*, Verlag Jena 1800, Berlin 2007

"Here I stand at the milestone of my days ♥ Marlene 1901–1992"

Never forgotten: Her beauty, her voice, her integrity

Maiden

atmospheres

The maiden has left a lasting mark on Berlin's cityscape in many different ways. There's obviously something important about the figure of the young or virginal woman. The "Jungfernbrücke," or Maiden's Bridge, in the Mitte district, is said to be where a Huguenot family (→ Fisimatenten) blessed with many unmarried daughters set up their market stall. The daughters soon became famous as the biggest gossips in Berlin. Today it's rare for young chatterboxes to find their way to this discreet and dignified spot behind the Ministry of Foreign Affairs.

The "Jungfernmühle," or Maiden's Mill, in Britz commemorates a sad story. The miller's daughter was killed by one of the windmill's vanes, and her father had her portrait carved into an oakwood panel below the mill shaft as a memorial.

Whether the beautiful blue love-in-a-mist flower, dubbed "maid in the greenery" in German, can be found in the "Jungfernheide," or Maiden's Heath park, would be worth finding out. The park is close by the avenue named Nonnendammallee (→ Nuns) and can be reached via the Jungfernheideweg, the street passing Jungfernheide Pond. Is there some connection between those nuns and the maidens?

The significance of virginity in patriarchal family units is a much less poetic affair. As a symbol of family honor, itself associated with control over girls and women, virginity has given rise to myths and rituals, tears and anxieties, sometimes to decisions over life and death (→ Honor). There have always been tricks to simulate an intact hymen, nowadays sometimes resorting to surgical techniques. But the "virgin" won't be put to rest as a thing of the past until we have complete gender equality, including cultural and sexual equality between women and men.

Location
Jungfernbrücke,
Oberwasserstrasse 11,
10117 Berlin

How to get there
U 2 Spittelmarkt

Maiden's Bridge, maiden's sigh, gentle mist, long shadows

Multiculti

atmospheres

Although Berlin was destroyed, divided, and ceased to be the capital of all of Germany after the war, the city's magnetism attracted people from near and far through all the vicissitudes in its history. West Berlin was a preferred destination for students, small-town-phobics, conscientious objectors, artists of all kinds, as well as the *Gastarbeiter*, or guest workers as they were called then, women and men from southern Europe and Turkey (➤ **Almancilar**); East Berlin was the gathering place for functionaries from Saxony, students, young men and women working in construction, as well as political refugees from Chile, and men and women from Vietnam (➤ **Under the bamboo roof**), Cuba, and Africa who had been hired as contract workers.

After the fall of ➤ **The Wall** young people came streaming into the metropolis of creativity and spontaneity. The new workforce of the capital was comprised of government civil servants, lobbyists, and investors. Ethnic Germans from the former Soviet Union (➤ **Russian Disco**) and war refugees from the former Yugoslavia came to the city, as well as extended families from Lebanon, masters in the art of survival from Poland, and countless girls and women from Eastern Europe in search of work and happiness (➤ **Working girls,** ➤ **Red-light**).

In late 2008 there were women from more than 188 different countries registered in Berlin as foreign nationals: 165,775 from other parts of Europe, 6,640 from Africa, 12,693 from the Americas, 34,801 from Asia, and even 890 from Oceania. No reliable statistics are available on the many immigrants who have already been naturalized. But there are a lot!

Location
Mehrgenerationenhaus Reinickendorf,
Auguste-Viktoria-Allee 17,
13403 Berlin

How to get there
U 8 Kurt-Schumacher-Platz,
Bus M 21, 122 Auguste-Viktoria-Allee / Humboldtstrasse

Multigenerational house: With a love for the multicultural details

Multiculti

atmospheres

Location
Karneval der Kulturen,
Friedrichshain-Kreuzberg

Russian, Polish, and Turkish neighborhoods have long since started leaving a mark on everyday life in Berlin. At the annual Carnival of Cultures, multicultural Berlin presents itself as particularly colorful and attractive.

Multiculti is neither good nor bad. Multiculti is reality. People of many different nationalities live here and that changes the lives of both the long-time residents and the newcomers. The intensive discourse about coexistence in the city, about immigration, assimilation, and language acquisition, show that this poses a major challenge for everyone. Encounters change everyone involved. But the conditions must be clearly defined.

Finding a balance between religious tolerance, cultural diversity, and the unrestricted validity of the Basic Law is especially controversial. It is no coincidence that the rights of women are often at the center of debate. Traditional, cultural, and religious ideas of patriarchal societies in fact often clearly contradict the equal rights guaranteed women in the Basic Law. For this reason, every declaration in support of diversity is also a declaration in support of equal rights, of the right of girls and women to attend school without restrictions, to choose their own partner, to be protected from family violence, to freely choose their religion and lifestyle, and it expresses a commitment to support them in exercising these rights. That is the true alternative to having parallel societies and spheres outside the protection of the Basic Law.

127

Carnival of Cultures—Small man very large: a popular dream everywhere

Painting ladies

atmospheres

It sounds derogatory, calling them "painting ladies"! Back then no one would have thought of calling a male artist a "painting gentleman." These female artists around the turn of the twentieth century had to tolerate this epithet since people simply didn't believe they had the ability to create art. Creative genius was defined as an exclusively male quality. Women who at that time wanted to work as professional artists not only violated social norms; they also faced the problem of how to receive training, as before the Weimar Republic women were denied admission to the official art academies, also in Berlin.

But the *painting ladies* did become outstanding artists, as evidenced by names such as Käthe Kollwitz (→ **Pietà**) and Paula Modersohn-Becker, Hannah Höch (→ **Dada**) and Lotte Laserstein, Jeanne Mammen and an artist who had been forgotten until early 2000, Clara Siewert, who died in 1944 in an air raid on Berlin that also destroyed most of her works. The 1987 catalogue *Das Verborgene Museum—Dokumentation der Kunst von Frauen in Berlin öffentlichen Sammlungen* (The Hidden Museum—Documentation of Art by Women in Public Collections in Berlin) remains the most relevant reference on female painters in Berlin. At the same time this reveals the fact that most works by women are—still today—not in exhibitions, but archives (→ **Clio**). Since it was founded in 1986, Das Verborgene Museum (The Hidden Museum) has created exhibitions and publications, presenting an interested audience with the works and lives of around a hundred female artists of the modern era.

Location
Das Verborgene Museum,
Schlüterstrasse 70, 10625 Berlin

How to get there
S 5, 7, 75, 9 Savignyplatz

Sources
Cornelia Carstens, Margret Luikenga, and Stephanie von Ow, *Immer den Frauen nach!*, ed. Berliner Geschichtswerkstatt e.V., Berlin, 1993

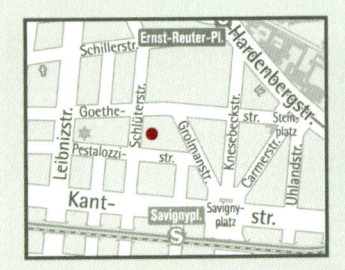

www.museumsportal-berlin.de
www.berlin-judentum.de

To find out more
Kerstin Merkel and Heide Wunder (eds), *Ungewöhnliche Frauen. Deutsche Dichterinnen, Malerinnen, Mäzeninnen aus vier Jahrhunderten*, Munich: Piper Verlag, 2007

Not the muse but the artist—a courageous affront to bourgeois sensibilities

Polionauts ...

atmospheres

... thalidothugs and blind flyers. Stop! Don't panic! Don't call the police! We're not a gang of criminals, but that doesn't mean we aren't dangerous—because we defend ourselves against being patronized and having others make decisions for us and we demand our rights. Anyone who thinks we are astronauts is also wrong, but we can be found along the approach corridor of Tempelhof Airport and we often do take off. Then we free ourselves from the chains of prejudice and heteronomy, represent our own interests, have fun, and do whatever we wish.

Because we are strong! Many of us didn't know that for a long time. And with most of us, it isn't apparent at first glance.

We are always happy when we manage to reel in more girls and women with the most varied disabilities from all of Berlin. With us they have the chance to raise a ruckus at events, confuse advisors, or show the other women their strengths.

And so we continue to become more and more polionauts, thalidothugs, and blind flyers—or how would you refer to yourself? In any case, one thing is clear: We are strong on our own, but together we are unbeatable!

Location
Disused runway, Tempelhof Airport, near Leinestrasse 27/28, 12049 Berlin

How to get there
U 8 Leinestrasse

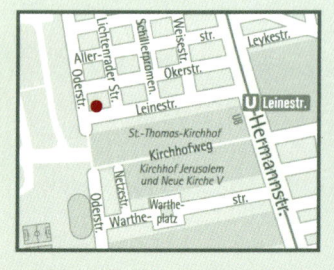

Source
www.netzwerk-behinderter-
 frauen-berlin.de

To find out more
Netzwerk behinderter Frauen
 Berlin e.V.,
 Leinestrasse 51, 12049 Berlin

Runway for those on a roll

Russian disco

atmospheres

Olga Kaminer came to Berlin with her family in 1990, when East Germany still existed. It was her husband Wladimir who started the sweat-inducing Russian Disco, which rang in a new phase of Russophilia in the city. There is a tradition to Russians in Berlin: Jewish emigrants who fled the pogroms of Tsarist Russia settled here; and White Guardists, aristocrats, and the intelligentsia, who escaped before the Russian Revolution, settled especially in the Charlottenburg district, which thus got the nickname Charlottengrad.

When the Red Army took over the city in 1945, for most of the women in Berlin this meant both liberation and unspeakable suffering. They paid for the victory over the Nazis with mass rape, which in the tradition of male warfare was both a war trophy and a means of humiliating the defeated adversary. The women remained silent—in the East due to politics and in the West for reasons of family morality. The former were not permitted to refer to the victors as rapists, and the latter were threatened with feelings of shame for the injustice done to them.

These were not the best conditions for reconciliation and coming together again. In East Germany the soldiers of the big brother were protected. In the West the anti-Soviet propaganda flourished. Berlin women never totally lost their skepticism. Nevertheless, after the fall of the Berlin Wall, the city offered a new home to roughly 100,000 ethnic Germans from the Soviet Union. While the women were generally well-educated and able to become integrated rather quickly, the men had more difficulty coming to terms with the demands of life in the Federal Republic of Germany. This divergence within the families added to the problem. For many, the happy and optimistic Russian Disco remains nothing but a dream.

Location
Deutsch-Russisches Museum,
Berlin-Karlshorst,
Zwieseler Strasse 4, 10318 Berlin

How to get there
S 3 Karlshorst

Sources
Rosemarie Schumann, *Fremde Heimat*, Berlin: Verlag am Park, 2003
Thomas Urban, *Russische Schriftsteller im Berlin der zwanziger*

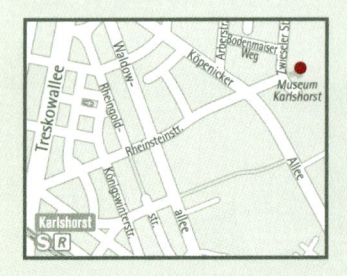

Jahre, Berlin: Nicolaische Verlagsbuchhandlung, 2003

Karl Schlögel, *Das russische Berlin. Ostbahnhof Europas*, Munich: Pantheon, 2007

To find out more

Wladimir Kaminer, *Russian Disco*, trans. Michael Hulse, London: Ebury Press, 2002

StattReisen "Charlottengrad – Russisches Leben in Berlin" www.007-berlin.de

"Home!" says the tank. But where's home?

travails

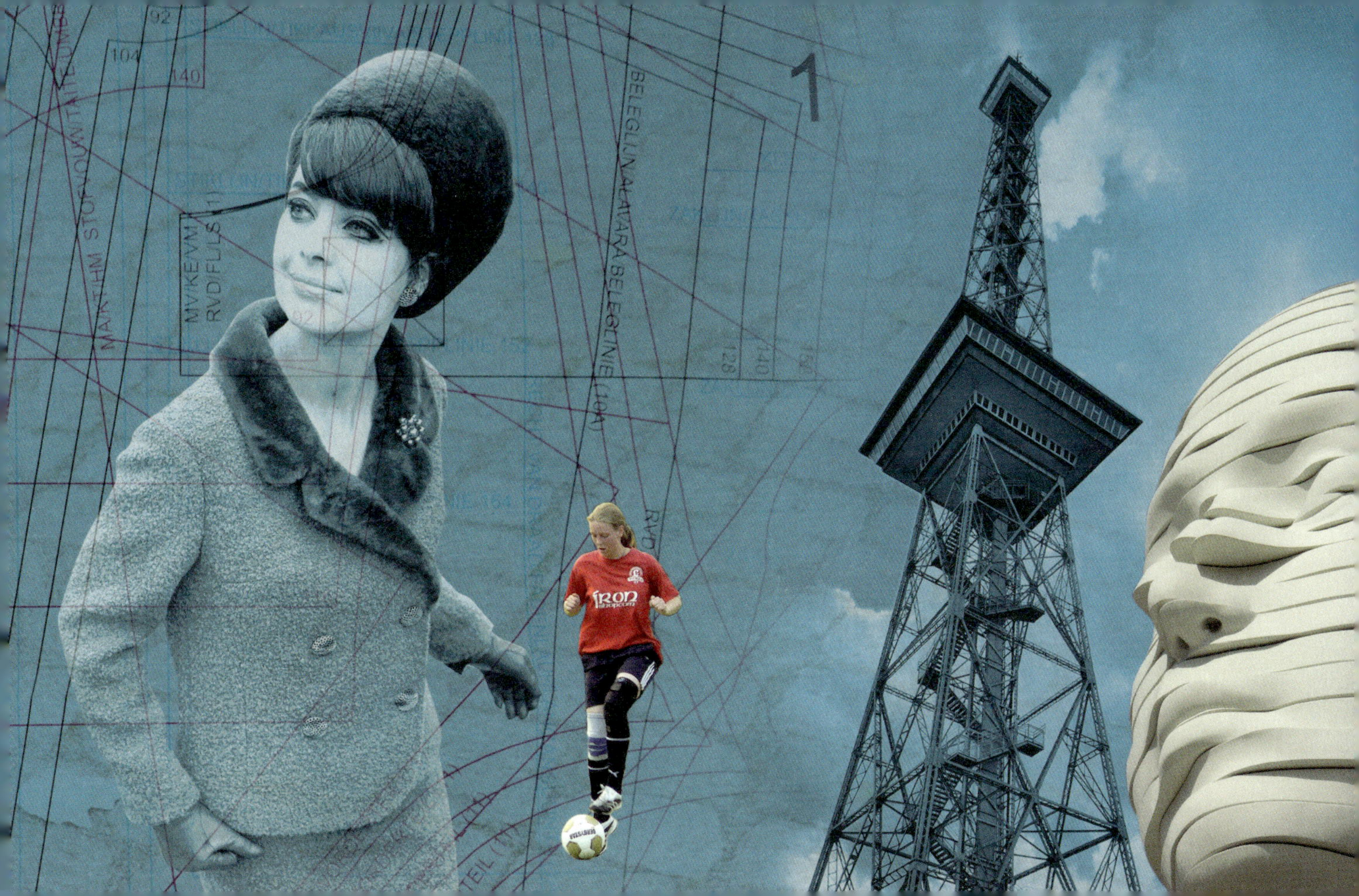
92
104
140
1
Iron

Alex

travails

Alexanderplatz, the traffic hub in the proletarian eastern part of the city, made such an impression on Grete Weiskopf (1905–1966), a young author from Salzburg, that in 1928 she assumed the nom de plume Alex Wedding. "Alex" after the famous square, and "Wedding" after the working-class district known as "Red Wedding." That much enthusiastic identification is unusual, even for Berlin. As a sign of her appreciation, Alex gave the city an extraordinary book.

The story of *Ede und Unku* (1931, Ede and Unku) tells of social hardship and childlike solidarity in the 1920s. A twelve-year-old boy Ede, whose father is unemployed, meets Unku, a Sinti girl, at a fair. He is impressed by the unconventional Unku, who even smokes a cigar sometimes and has her own idea of what's yours and what's mine. Ede delivers newspapers to add to the rather tight family budget and Unku helps him with a horse and cart. For that he is teased and ridiculed by the other newspaper boys. He hopes that a bicycle will help him gain some acceptance from them, but it proves to be nothing but wishful thinking. However, Unku grifts some money and gets him a bicycle. This confirms the prejudices of the adults, and Ede, too, doesn't understand his friend at first.

The Nazis threw the book onto the bonfire at the book-burning in 1933. Alex Wedding could escape to New York. Erna Lauenberger, the model for Unku, and her two children were killed as ➔ **Gypsies** in Auschwitz. After the war the book became standard reading in schools in East Germany.

Alex Wedding is today considered the founder of proletarian children's literature. Berlin's Academy of Fine Arts awards an Alex Wedding Prize every two or three years for children's and young people's books. And Alex, the square, is still the poor relative, not very chic, but full of life.

Location
Alexanderplatz, 10178 Berlin

How to get there
S-Bahn and U-Bahn Alexanderplatz,
Bus TXL, M 48, 100, 200, 248,
Tram M 2, M 4, M 5, M 6

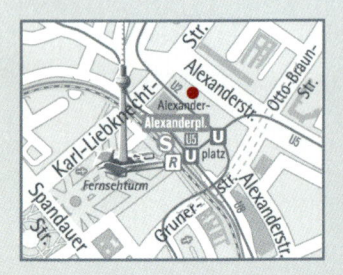

Sources
http://de.wikipedia.org/wiki/
  Grete_Weiskopf
www.amadeu-antonio-stiftung.de

To find out more
Harald Hauswald, *Alexanderplatz. Fotografische und literarische Erinnerungen*, Berlin: Jaron Verlag, 2007

No matter what's built on it, Alex remains Alex.

Berlin air

travails

Whether the theme of a popular song or sought-after in the city for its promise of freedom, until a few years ago the real Berlin air was anything but praiseworthy. Industry, coal heating, and growing car traffic were a source of stench, filth, and hazardous levels of toxins. Today the snow stays white for weeks, which is incredible compared to the black grunge of the 1980s. For Berlin's air, the interplay of industrial decline, conversion to cleaner heating systems, and exhaust filters has been a blessing—also for housewives and mothers, who were constantly battling dirt and disease. Berlin has established a "low emission zone," banning polluting vehicles from the city center; the worst of the filth is gone, but the hazard of fine particulate matter and CO_2 still needs to be dealt with.

Women should be setting environmental and traffic policies, as they are more critical of traffic, more sensitive to environmental threats, and more often confronted with the negative impact of pollution and noise in their everyday lives. Thus they could be real go-getters in demanding environmental protection. But women aren't the policymakers. There are very few women in high-responsibility administrative or government positions, even in environmental associations, despite their great concern for the environment.

The Association of Women Building Experts is working to change this. Its traveling exhibition "Prima Klima für Frauen" ("Perfect Climate for Women") on future-oriented careers in the climate sector explains how to combine one's career with environmental activism. It's the perfect labor market for women. A growing number of women are pioneering in mud-brick construction, guerilla gardening, and intercultural vegetable gardening projects, offering hope for Berlin's climate.

Location
Berliner Funkturm (Radio Tower),
Hammarskjöldplatz 1,
14057 Berlin

How to get there
S 41, 42 Messe Nord/ICC,
U 2 Theodor-Heuss-Platz

Sources

www.genanet.de
www.stadtentwicklung.berlin.de
www.baufachfrau-berlin.de
www.berlingoesgreen.de

The blue sky above Berlin—simply beautiful!

Business by and for women

travails

Women create jobs for themselves and other women. They run businesses and start up new ones. Women's businesses are more stable than those run by men because women tend to take less financial risks. In terms of economic and labor market policies, businesses run by women make a lot of sense, so they are becoming increasingly common (➤ **Gold Rush**).

Together instead of alone—a neighborhood of various women's businesses that profit from one another not only through moral support but also in a business sense: This appears to be what women are seeking. Set up on 75,000 sq. feet for fifty businesswomen in a prime location in Berlin's city center, the WeiberWirtschaft, founded in 1994, is the first, largest, and most elaborate center for businesses owned and run by women in Germany—with stores, trades and services, and restaurants. Smaller centers have followed in the districts of Neukölln, Friedrichshain-Kreuzberg, and Marzahn-Hellersdorf. The second-largest center for start-ups by women opened its doors in 2005, with more than 30,000 sq. feet of space for 44 businesses: UCW, the Charlottenburg-Wilmersdorf Women's Business Center.

Location
Unternehmerinnen- und Gründerinnenzentrum Charlottenburg-Wilmersdorf (UCW),
Sigmaringer Strasse 1,
10713 Berlin

How to get there
U 7 Blissestrasse, Bus 101, 104, 249
U-Bahnhof Blissestrasse

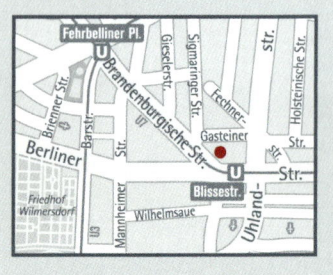

To find out more
www.ucw-berlin.de
Frauenwirtschaftszentrum
  Neukölln in the Kindl Boulevard,
  Hermannstrasse 214–216,
  12049 Berlin
www.hafen-gruenderinnen.de
www.frauennetzwerkkreuzberg.de
www.weiberwirtschaft.de

Caterpillar, cobra, columbine

travails

What does all this flora and fauna have to do with women? The founders of the Raupe und Schmetterling (Caterpillar and Butterfly) organization for women in the middle of their lives view their name as their aim. After all, the transformation of a caterpillar into a butterfly symbolizes the chance for a metamorphosis, a comprehensive, profound change sought by many women in their middle years. And the butterfly is a symbol of freedom, ease, and lightheartedness.

So that's what it's about. Women freeing themselves of constraints, burdens, and obligations. They want to leave the well-tread roads and seek new pathways, whether it is a new career orientation, career re-entry, or an attempt at self-employment, or finally to satisfy a dream long set aside, or maybe to shed light on relationships and partnerships and decide: It this good for me? Some women are planning a residential community or considering doing volunteer work. Or letting their children become independent and learning to let go.

Our culture does not have many role models with respect to women's processes of change. Wherever women venture to make a new start, to unfold their wings or shed their skin, valuable rudiments emerge for a culture of a self-confident female transformation. In any case, neither burnout nor midlife crisis can be considered a desirable alternative.

Kobra (cobra) and Akelei (European columbine) are other organizations that offer career counseling for women. Meeting places such as all of these offer assistance, networking, and counseling in difficult life situations. Cats might have nine lives; women have just one—but it's long ...

Location
Schmetterlingshaus der Naturschutzstation Malchow e.V., Dorfstrasse 35, 13051 Berlin

How to get there
Bus 154, 259 Malchow/Dorfstrasse

To find out more

www.raupeundschmetterling.de
www.kobra-berlin.de
www.akelei-online.de
www.ucw-berlin.de
www.isi-ev.de
www.hafen-gruenderinnen.de
www.weiberwirtschaft.de

Why not learn from the butterflies?

Girls from the office

travails

The legendary telephone operator stands for the phenomenon of a career for working women that developed in the 1920s. Women worked before that time, such as seamstress homeworkers (➜ Treadling like crazy), housekeepers, maids, and female servants of all kinds (➜ Working girls), as well as countless workers who toiled in the factories during Berlin's early industrialization. But new was the social status of the female employee who was independent, since she had her own income and rented her own apartment or at least a furnished room. The mostly single young women went dancing or to the movies, drove out to the countryside, and even did sports—and they didn't give a hoot that the older generation thought that was unseemly (➜ Amazon). Accordingly, they wore pants and shorter skirts—and hair: the bob celebrated its heyday. The young women smoked, went to cafés and restaurants, theaters and cabarets, and then on Monday went back to work in the office, the shop, or, yes, at the telephone switchboard. The new woman had been born—and for the never idle conservatives of the Weimar Republic she would become the new bugbear symbolizing cultural decline and degeneracy. Literature and film, on the other hand, celebrated the new heroines, who were also worthy of wooing as consumers: Mascha Kaléko (1907–1975) and her *Lyrisches Stenogrammheft* (Lyrical Steno-Notebook), Irmgard Keun (1905–1982) and *Das kunstseidene Mädchen* (The Artificial Silk Girl). Titles like Destinies behind Typewriters, Girls from the Office, or The Girl at the Orga Typewriter all illustrate the fascinating aura of these independent, androgynous-looking women.

Location
Postfuhramt (Old Post Office), Oranienburger Strasse 35/36, 10117 Berlin

How to get there
S1, S2, S25, U6 Oranienburger Strasse, Tram M1, M6, 12, 50 Oranienburger Tor, Bus 240

Sources
Siegfried Kracauer, *The Salaried Masses: Duty and Distraction in*

Weimar Germany, trans. Quintin Hoare, London: Verso, 1998 [German: 1930]

To find out more
Irmgard Keun, *The Artificial Silk Girl*, trans. Katharina von Ankum, New York: Other Press, 2002 [German: 1932]
Vicky Baum, *Grand Hotel*, trans. Basil Creighton. Garden City, NY: Doubleday, 1931 [German: 1929]

Architectural communication: The post office dome greets the synagogue dome across the street

Gold rush

travails

The idea was for women to invest in women. The symbol was a female pearl diver, who stands for the courage of women to go their own way. Sometimes that demands more than just perseverance and creativity; sometimes it demands financial backing.

The women from Goldrausch (gold rush) dreamed of golden times: a guaranteed basic income, paid work, and economic independence. A first step was a solidarity network that started in 1982 with anonymous donations totaling about 200,000 deutschmarks. It was to support women starting businesses. All in all, over the years more than 450 women's businesses have received financial subsidies amounting to roughly €800,000.

Criteria for receiving funding have always been to: employ exclusively women in the company; engage in no sexist, racist, or environmentally harmful activities; have the seat of the company in Berlin; and also seek matched funding. The applications for funding are discussed and recipients are selected in meetings open to the public.

The level of funds paid back is very high, owing to social controls and the consensus of all participants not to waste, much less misappropriate, their shared money. Presently, about €12,000 in loans and €3,000 in subsidies are awarded annually. The funds are administered to a large extent on a volunteer basis. Over the years, the work has become increasingly professionalized; there is a network with other small loan initiatives that have meanwhile been started, as well as with women experts from politics and industry and with banks and organizations for new businesses (→ Public money).

Location
Goldrausch Frauennetzwerk e.V.,
Potsdamer Strasse 139,
10783 Berlin

How to get there
U 2 Bülowstrasse,
Bus M 48 U-Bahnhof Bülowstrasse

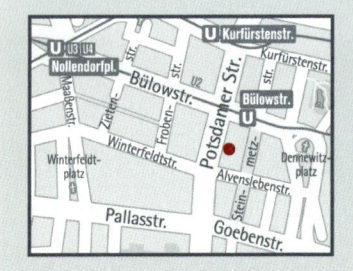

Source

Birgit Daiber and Ricarda Buch, *Risikoexistenz Frau. Zur Geschichte von Frauennetzwerken und Frauen betrieben in Berlin*, Berlin: Inselpresse Lindwerder, 2007

To find out more
www.goldrausch-ev.de

Goldrausch's small steps to the Berlin stock exchange's massive stance

Mannequins

travails

When you enter the subway at the Hausvogteiplatz station, you are immediately confronted with the history of this location. A wall of mirrors reflects nineteen plates set into the station steps with names of Jewish garment manufacturers who lived here until they were driven out by the Nazis. Starting in 1836 Hausvogteiplatz was the heart of Berlin's fashion industry, as clothing was one of Berlin's main export items (➜ Treadling like crazy).

The Nazi regime destroyed the century-old fashion tradition at this site: Jewish ready-made garment factories were Aryanized and their owners either emigrated or were deported. Four thousand people who had worked around Hausvogteiplatz were deported and murdered.

Not until the fall of ➜ The Wall did Berlin once again become a creative fashion location, though no longer at Hausvogteiplatz. But one of the typical fashion atelier buildings of the heyday there is still standing at no. 3–4 (Haus am Bullenwinkel).

The atmosphere of change in the 1990s and Berlin's relative affordability attracted a lot of artisans to the city. Some eight hundred fashion designers have meanwhile settled here. Paris might still be more elegant, and Milan classier, and London hipper, but with the so-called Berlin style, whose secret is not having any particular style at all, Berlin is reclaiming its reputation as an international fashion capital. Today's models, stylized to the point of lifelessness (➜ Ideal), have more in common with mannequins than is apparent at first glance. *Männeken*, the German word for both model and mannequin, derived from the French *mannequin* and English *manikin*, can be traced back to the Dutch *manneken*, meaning "little man," which was originally nothing more than a jointed doll.

Location
Hausvogteiplatz, 10117 Berlin

How to get there
U 2 Hausvogteiplatz

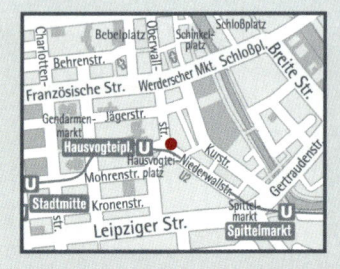

Sources

Uwe Westphal: *Berliner Konfektion und Mode 1836–1939. Die Zerstörung einer Tradition*, Berlin: Edition Hentrich, 1992

Eva Kosack, Ingrid Kuntzsch, and Ilse Laatz-Krumnow: *Jugendlexikon Kleider und Mode*, Bibliographisches Institut Leipzig 1986

Katja Aschke (ed.): *Kleider machen viele Leute. Mode machen – aber wie?* Reinbek: Rowohlt, 1989

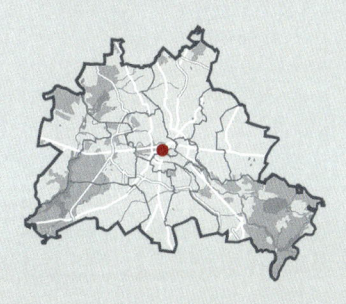

No reflections in the mirrors. Fashion has sought out new venues.

No special treatment

travails

They saw, solder, hammer, sweep chimneys, repair cars, and tile roofs: Women have long since entered the trades. Day after day they dismantle the argument raised by businesses that women always need special treatment. Fear of female troublemakers on construction sites is subsiding. The Berlin Chamber of Skilled Crafts has been recording a steady increase in the share of women in its membership, helping Berlin to continually top the list in Germany. With the rise in women entrepreneurs, executives, skilled staff, or apprentices, the male-dominated trades have started to totter. One third of the apprentices in Berlin crafts are female, and the trend is rising. For all of Germany the figure is almost one in four. But not only the number of female trainees is rising—so is their level of education: 12.4 percent have university entrance qualifications, compared with only 5.9 percent of their male counterparts.

The annual Practical Achievement competition sponsored by the German Association of Young Craftspeople also reflects the above-average achievements of the women. Although only roughly one third of the apprentices in Berlin are women, they comprise about half the state winners.

Berlin's Competence Center for Craftswomen offers valuable assistance to women in the trades. It works to secure and expand equal opportunities for craftswomen, who have chosen their career out of conviction. Individual personnel development provisions for craftswomen and companies, as well as continuing training opportunities to expand areas of competence, and targeted publicity all serve to promote the career opportunities for women in the trades and to strengthen the image of women in the trades and in the public eye.

Location
Rixdorfer Schmiede (blacksmith's shop), Master craftswoman Gabriele Sawitzky,
Richardplatz 28, 12055 Berlin

How to get there
U 7 Karl-Marx-Strasse,
S 41, 42 Sonnenallee

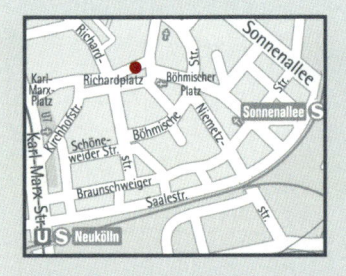

Source

Handwerkskammer Berlin:
 www.hwk-berlin.de

To find out more

www.frauenimhandwerk.de

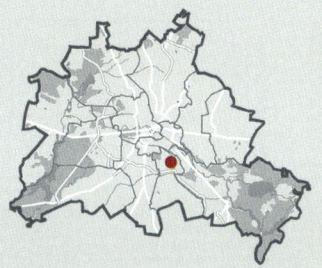

A trade in hand finds gold in every land—also for women.

Soccer

travails

Germany is world champion! At least regarding the women. For them, the title has almost become routine. Society and soccer club charters are lagging behind a bit. As recently as 1989 the German Soccer Association (DFB) found it appropriate to award the European women's soccer champs with a coffee service. Was it intended as a beautiful dowry to improve the players' marriage prospects? Considering the bad reputation they have …

For the 2007 World Cup victory, at least, the prize was €50,000 per player—not quite the €250,000 victory premium for the men, but at least the award was no longer in kind. In terms of economic history, this finally marked the end of serfdom. But it does not yet satisfy demands for equal pay for equal work, the classic battle of the women's movement. There is still much room for improvement.

Soccer and men go together here like bread and butter. The first women in Germany who tried their luck at the growing working-class sport received jeers and scorn. Things are different in the United States. American football is considered the archetypical men's sport there, so soccer was not appropriated by men and was instead left to the women. Despite the guarantee of equality in Germany's Basic Law, the male world of soccer succeeded in making it virtually impossible for women to play here, and in the 1950s they were even banned from playing! Not until 1970 did the DFB reluctantly lift the ban due to national and international pressure. Women played anyway, but *without* recognition, money, or support. More than a million ball-kicking girls and women, and international victories, have slowly turned things around. Since 2010 there is a DFB-sponsored cup final for women, and in 2011 the soccer World Cup for women has been held in Germany. Things are looking up.

Location
"Am Fennpfuhl" soccer field,
Storkower Strasse 209,
10369 Berlin

How to get there
S 41, 42, 8 Storkower Strasse,
Bus 156, 240 Paul-Junius-Strasse

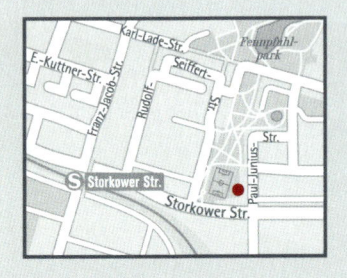

Sources
www.fansoccer.de
www.berliner-fussball.de

To find out more
Olympiastadion (Olympic stadium), Olympischer Platz 3, 14053 Berlin
Eduard Hoffmann and Jürgen Nendza, *Verlacht, verboten und gefeiert. Zur Geschichte des Frauenfussballs in Deutschland*, Weilerswist: Verlag Landpresse, 2006

Getting out of the offside trap

Social work

travails

She wrote her dissertation in 1908 on the causes for unequal pay for work done by men or by women. Today women are still making their demands heard on Equal Pay Day. But when Alice Salomon (1872–1948) received her doctorate on this subject, major areas of education and employment for women were truly uncharted, even forbidden territory.

As a daughter from a well-to-do family she already had gone through a tormenting period of idle waiting. She couldn't become a teacher for class reasons. Her social involvement in the bourgeois women's movement opened up other paths for her. The women's movement saw hardship not as an individual's plight, but due to strict separation of social classes and exploitation (→ Suppenlina). In this spirit, middle-class social reformers opened hostels for young women and a working women's club near Jannowitz Bridge. They advocated financial and psychological support for single mothers. They fought against child labor and high infant mortality rates, and for better hygienic conditions, 10-hour workdays, and support for new mothers.

Alice Salomon soon assumed a leading role in women's welfare activities. Influenced by the British approach of empirical social research, she founded Germany's first women's school for social work in 1908 in Berlin's Schöneberg district. Previously women could not take the university entrance exam and study at certain institutions of higher learning. Alice Salomon professionalized social work and thus created a new profession and source of work for women. Unfortunately, it has remained a women's domain with comparatively low status and poor pay. Since 1991 the University of Applied Sciences for Social Work and Social Education, which has since moved to Marzahn-Hellersdorf, bears the name of its founder.

Location
Alice Salomon Hochschule,
Alice-Salomon-Platz 5,
12627 Berlin

How to get there
U 5 Hellersdorf

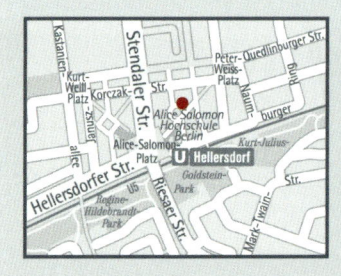

Source
www.ash-berlin.eu

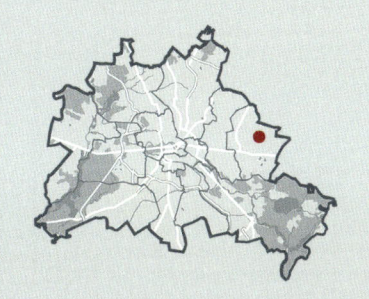

155

Social work is now taught at three universities in Berlin.

The milkmaid's calculations

travails

They delivered milk and could add complex prices on their fingers, those milkmaids of the Bolle dairy in Berlin. But the daydreaming milkmaid still has a bad reputation. Maybe because of Aesop's fable: The farmer's daughter was walking to market with a pail of milk on her head. Calculating in her head what she'd do with her earnings from the milk, her imagination got the best of her. She'd buy eggs, which would hatch into chickens, which she could sell to buy a fancy dress to wear at a dance. When young admirers spoke to her, she'd toss her head grandly and walk away. As she tossed her head in her daydream, she spilled the milk and her calculations were all for naught.

The mathematical prejudice is persistent: Boys are good at math; girls aren't. Period. Of course that isn't true. First, young boys and girls can add equally well—math aptitudes don't diverge until around age 15. Second, girls are worse at arithmetic if they sense that is expected of them. This is most pronounced when femininity and math are considered incompatible. Third, girls in other cultures, especially in Asia, show a similar skill level in arithmetic as boys. A weakness in math is thus caused by prejudice—which needs to be countered.

Math also opens doors to fascinating careers. On Girls' Day, companies such as the Solon solar module manufacturers, Alba waste management, Siemens engineering conglomerate, and Berlin Chemie pharmaceuticals invite girls to gain insight into technical and scientific jobs. The MINT For You initiative also encourages enjoyment of *M*ath, *I*nformation sciences, *N*atural sciences, and *T*echnology. Women studying or teaching at Berlin universities offer introductory courses to open girls' eyes to the many careers in the natural sciences. Smart girls sum it up quickly: it pays.

Location
"Heads, shifting," sculpture by Josefine Günschel and Margund Smolka, Forumsplatz on the Adlershof Campus of the Humboldt University of Berlin, Rudower Chaussee, 12489 Berlin

How to get there
S 45, 46, 8, 9 Adlershof

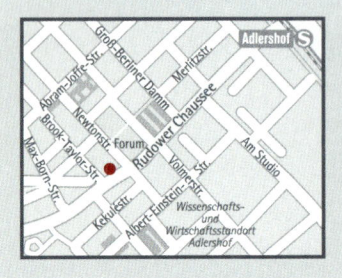

Sources
www.mintzukunft.de
www.girls-day.de

To find out more
www.planet-beruf.de
www.adlershof.hu-berlin.de/
   standort/koepfe

Math isn't only for milkmaids.

Treadling like crazy *travails*

By the late 19th century Berlin had become a center of the German garment industry (→ Mannequins). Work was done both in factories and by homeworkers; piecework done at home was a women's job, and the worst paid in the industry. In addition, the homeworkers' meager earnings had to suffice to finance their sewing machine and thread as well. The women spent twelve or more hours a day at their treadle sewing machines, which gave them the nickname *Trampeltier* in Berlin dialect, since they were trampling on that foot pedal all day. And on top of that many also had to take care of their children.

One of them was Agnes Wabnitz. She came to Berlin in 1870 and started sewing coats as a homeworker so she could also care for her mother. She came from a family that had once been well-off, she received good schooling, was interested in politics, and came to be a talented speaker. She knew the problems women faced first hand and could put into words the things that common people were thinking. She encouraged women to become organized to make their interests and problems heard. With humor and irony she opposed the church and public authorities, for which she received a number of jail sentences and fines. State prosecutors attempted to have her legally incapacitated in order to counter her growing popularity among the working class. When she was supposed to go to jail yet again on August 28, 1894, she committed suicide at a symbolic site, the cemetery dedicated to those killed in the March Revolution of 1848. Agnes Wabnitz's funeral became a political demonstration, although police had banned a funeral procession through the city. More than 60,000 mourners came and 630 wreaths were laid at her grave. That was eighty more than were laid at the funeral services for Kaiser Wilhelm I.

Location
Grave at the Friedhof der Freireligiösen Gemeinde, Pappelallee 15–17, 10437 Berlin

How to get there
U 2 Eberswalder Strasse

Sources
Claudia von Gélieu, "Achtzig Kränze mehr als der Kaiser," in *Spuren Suche. Frauen in Pankow, Prenzlauer Berg und Weissensee*, ed. Bezirksamt Pankow von Berlin, Berlin 2006

To find out more
Agnes-Wabnitz-Strasse (since 2000) in the Alter Schlachthof urban development area, 10249 Berlin, near S-Bahnhof Landsberger Allee

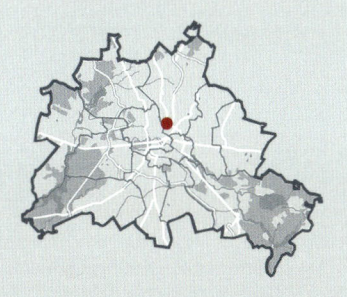

The secret empress of hearts

Washerwomen

travails

In the old days washing was hard work. The proverbial realm of the washerwomen was especially in Köpenick, where the soft water of the Spree and Dahme rivers was well-suited for washing laundry and the meadows could be used for bleaching and drying in the sun and wind (➤ **Out in the boondocks**).

Henriette Lustig was one of these washerwomen, and with her washing of bed and household linens and underclothes she became the first businesswoman in Köpenick. Mother Lustig, as she was called, received a permit to run a commercial laundry in 1835. Her residence at Alter Markt no. 4 is still standing.

Köpenick, particularly the Spindlersfeld section, was to remain Berlin's laundry room for more than 150 years. In Rewatex, a state-owned company in East Germany, clothing was washed, pressed, cleaned, and ironed. The work in steam and heat, with loud washing machine drums and huge rotary irons, was draining, and a career as a textile cleaning specialist was certainly no dream job. For this reason, the work at Rewatex was at times done by inmates of the East Berlin women's prisons (➤ **Green Minna**).

People could bring their dirty laundry to Rewatex drop-off locations and pick it up in clean packages a few days later. In the areas with new residential housing, this could also be done at the "complex collection point" (though you couldn't really get rid of any real complexes there!). The doorstep pick-up service that was initially set up was unfortunately discontinued rather quickly. The currently growing market for household-related services is perhaps an attempt to reintroduce this great idea. The Rewatex buildings are now an industrial ruin, in part protected as a historical landmark.

Location
"The Washerwoman," sculpture at the Frauentog, a small bay between Palace Island (Schlossinsel) Köpenick and Kietz

How to get there
Bus 167, Tram 61, 62, 67
Schlossplatz Köpenick

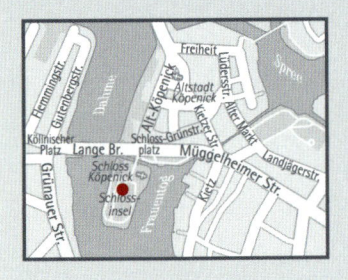

Source

Heimatverein Köpenick e. V. (ed.), *Von Copnic nach Köpenick. Ein Gang durch 800 Jahre Geschichte*, Berlin: trafoverlag, 2009

To find out more

Wäscherinnen (Washerwomen), DEFA documentary film by Jurgen Böttcher, East Germany, 1972

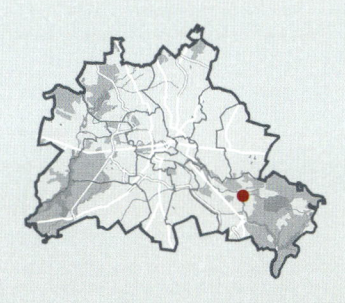

They wash and wash the whole day long.

Women at the helm

travails

A woman at the helm of local public transportation, whether a double-decker bus, a tram, subway (U-Bahn), or commuter rail (S-Bahn), is becoming a less and less of a rarity in Berlin. Although women still make up a small minority (about nine percent), a growing number of girls are showing an interest in training with the BVG, Berlin's public transportation system.

In 1940, when the men were at war, women first took the driver's seats of buses and trains. However, this development was turned around during the postwar years. Once work behind a steering wheel was again well paid, the jobs were held almost exclusively by men. Only in East Berlin, where the streetcar system was maintained and not replaced by buses as it was in the western sectors, were female streetcar and subway operators a familiar sight. In West Berlin, the first women were hired as drivers in 1973.

At the last count there were 337 women operating buses, streetcars, and subways for the BVG. As a result of dedicated efforts of women's interest organizations, meetings of the women drivers take place regularly to deal with issues such as equal opportunities, equal pay, and family-friendly policies of the company. A plan to promote women was devised and women were guaranteed the right to return to their workplace after maternity leave. Of the 897 S-Bahn drivers, sixty-one are women.

There are no women on the supervisory boards of either BVG or S-Bahn. And it was only in 2010 that Sigrid Nikutta became the first woman to head the BVG, though the S-Bahn top management still lacks women entirely. Of course, the management levels and corporate policies of these companies could certainly profit from the highly praised qualities of caution and the ability to deal with conflict that are often attributed to women.

Location
U-Bahnhof Residenzstrasse,
13409 Berlin

How to get there
U 8 Residenzstrasse

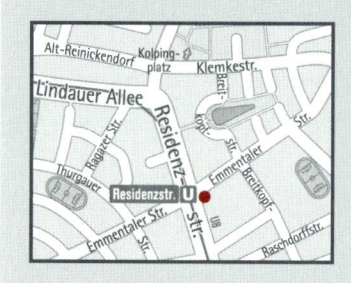

Sources
www.bvg.de
www.verdi.de
DB Mobility Logistic AG

To find out more
You too can drive a tram! BVG streetcar simulator, Ausbildungszentrum (training center), Siegfriedstrasse 30–35, 10365 Berlin, Tel.: +49 (30) 25 63 03 33

Rerouting the supervisory boards is on the women's policy timetable.

Korsett Engelke

tribulations

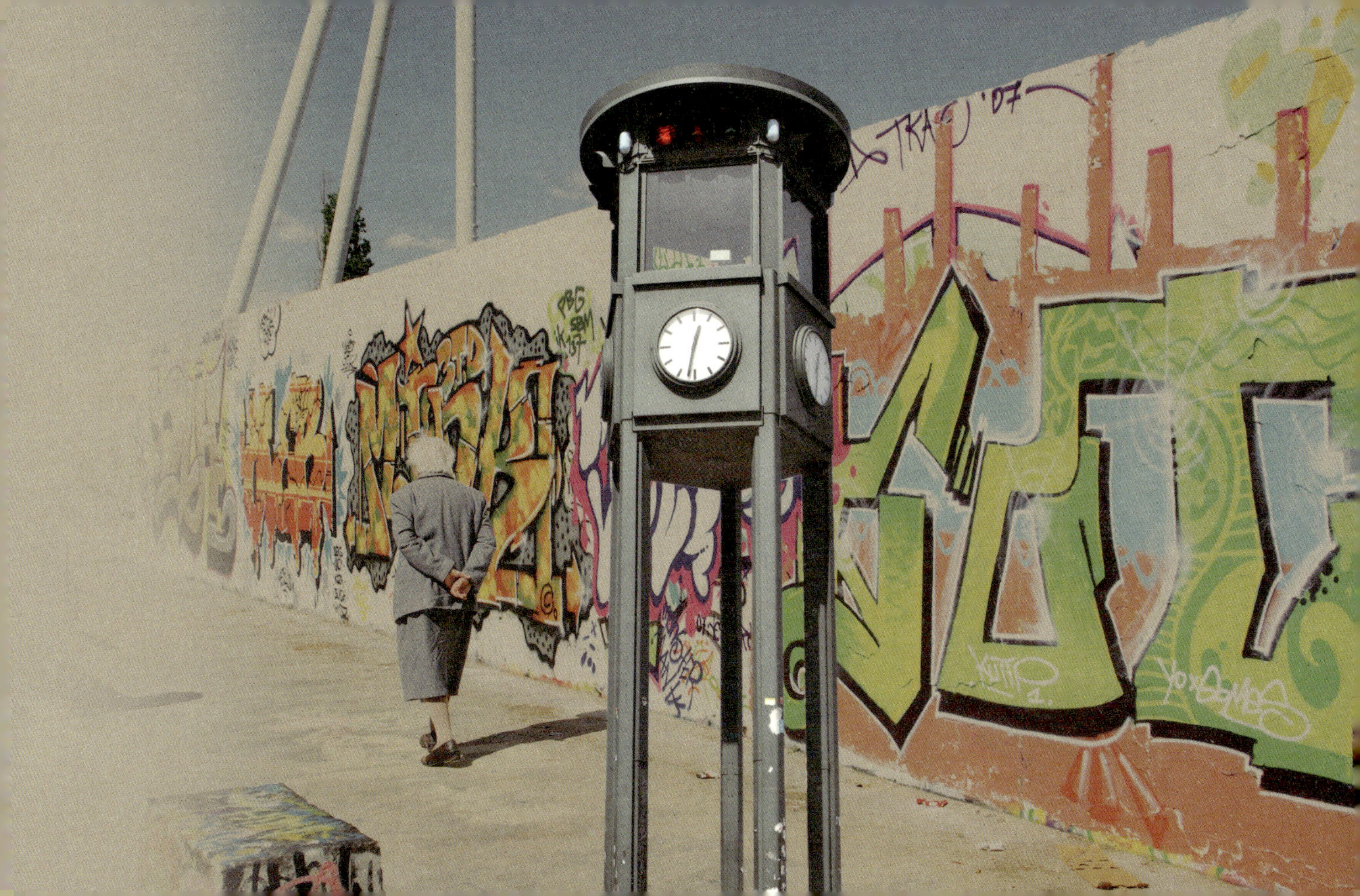

Baby of the family

tribulations

With blond braids and blue eyes, cheerful little Annemarie skips through the childlike imagination of generations of German girls and women. *Nesthäkchen*, the baby of the family, was the early-20th-century prototype of literature for teenage girls that was popular only in Germany. The ten-volume series between 1918 and 1925 reached an audience in the millions, proudly telling the story of seventy years of the heroine's life. Still today, far more than half the women who grew up in Germany know the *Nesthäkchen* books.

Nesthäkchen is a happy child, growing up in the idyll of a bourgeois physician's family in Wilhelmine Berlin. The patriarchy rules benevolently and caringly in these novels and the conservative bourgeoisie shows itself from its preferred side as a protector of values, culture, and good living. The Jewish background of the assimilated family disappears between Christmas trees, Easter eggs, and children's birthday parties with a few remaining religious traces. This idyll is based on gender roles and the novels tell the story of learning them. What girls are allowed to do and learn, and what they cannot; how hard work and selflessness can be combined, and that the horizons of the most wild girl end in the haven of matrimony—that is told enthusiastically and cheerfully.

The fact that the women's movement was fighting at the same time for the rights to education, suffrage, and employment was faintly visible in the series, but this new female momentum served only to uphold patriarchal society. Studying medicine? Yes, in order to help Papa in his practice and later to help the husband. A singing career? Yes, but only until she marries. Female intellect? Yes, but the head of the family, of course, has the last word. While German conservatives continue to mourn the loss of this idyll today, the best-seller author of the *Nesthäkchen*

Location
Else-Ury-Jugendbibliothek
(Young People's Library),
Glogauer Strasse 13, 10999 Berlin

How to get there
Bus M 29 Glogauer / Reichenberger Strasse

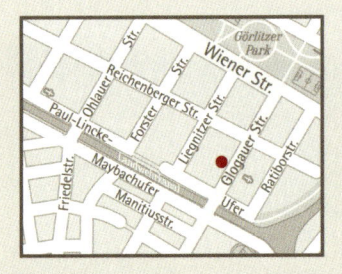

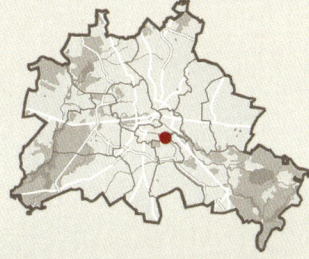

In the heart of Kreuzberg—a multicultural Else Ury

Baby of the family

tribulations

series, Else Ury, had to wait till the bitter end to see how the esteemed qualities of conservatism, nationalism, and patriotism would turn criminal. Even Nazi Germany did not want to do without the conservative image of women depicted in her novels. But it could do without the author. Irrespective of the ongoing success of her books she was not allowed to continue publishing after 1933, her income and property were expropriated, and her citizenship was revoked. She and her Jewish coreligionists were forced to endure more than 2,000 laws and ordinances of persecution, humiliation, and expropriation, conceived in the offices and legal and medical associations of the national-conservative middle class which she so highly valued.

In January 1943, Else Ury was deported from the assembly camp at Grosse Hamburger Strasse 26 to Auschwitz and sent immediately to the gas chamber, where she was murdered. She was sixty-five years old. Her suitcase was found in the Auschwitz memorial in 1995. There was never a "Nesthäkchen in Auschwitz" published as a book in the series.

To find out more

Memorial plaque at Kantstrasse 30, 10623 Berlin (Else Ury lived there from 1905 to 1932)

Weissensee Jewish Cemetery, Herbert-Baum-Strasse 45, 13088 Berlin

Else-Ury-Passage (The alleyway between Bleibtreu- and Knesebeckstrasse was named after Else Ury in 1999.)

Marianne Brentzel, *"Mir kann doch nichts geschehen…" Das Leben der Nesthäkchen-Autorin Else Ury*, Berlin: Edition Ebersbach, 2007

Jüdisches Museum, Lindenstrasse 9–14, 10969 Berlin

Gabriele Beyerlein, *In Berlin vielleicht*, Stuttgart: Thienemann, 2005

Gabriele Beyerlein, *Berlin, Bülowstrasse 80 a*, Stuttgart: Thienemann, 2007

Gabriele Beyerlein, *Es war in Berlin*, Stuttgart: Thienemann, 2009 (an exciting young people's book on the living conditions and emancipatory struggles of maids, middle-class daughters, and female nobility in the German Empire)

Book of the Poor

tribulations

Berlin still advertises itself as poor, but sexy. On the one hand, the sexiness of poverty is often nothing but exploitation in the sex business (→ Red-light). On the other hand is the long history of fighting poverty in the city. One of the many women who in the past worked to help Berlin's poor and weak was Bettina von Arnim née Brentano (1785–1859).

The public memory (→ Clio) knows Bettina von Arnim first and foremost as a writer of the Romantic period, as the sister and wife of famous writers of the Romantic, and as youthful and puckish. But she was one of the smartest political thinkers of her time. In her book *Das Buch gehört dem König* [The Book Belongs to the King] published in 1843 she described with clarity and passion the misery of people in the impoverished districts of the city. In order to avoid being censored, she made the very clever move to dedicate the book to Friedrich Wilhelm IV personally. Whether it was the Polish struggle for liberty, abolition of the death penalty, or emancipation of Jews and women, Bettina took a stand with her writing, even in the Restoration period after 1848. After her husband's death she also had to work hard to maintain her estate and support her large family.

Poverty continues to be a topical issue in Berlin. Especially the many single mothers and their children survive at the margins of subsistence. As in feudal times, they have to rely on soup kitchens and grocery donations. Even medical treatment of many homeless people or those living here illegally is in the hands of women doing volunteer work. They all know that in addition to charitable aid, it is necessary to redirect politics in order for efforts to end poverty to have any lasting impact.

Location
Gesundheitszentrum für Obdachlose (Health Center for the Homeless), Jenny De la Torre Stiftung, Pflugstrasse 12, 10115 Berlin

How to get there
U 6, Tram M 8 Schwartzkopffstrasse, Tram M 6 Pflugstrasse

Source

Anita Sachse, "Bettina von Arnim," in *SpurenSuche. Frauen in Pankow*, ed. Bezirksamt Pankow von Berlin, Berlin 2006

To find out more

Ursula Püschel, *Bettina von Arnim – politisch. Erkundungen, Entdeckungen, Erkenntnisse*, Bielefeld: Aisthesis Verlag, 2005, http://www.delatorre-stiftung.dedelatorre-stiftung.php/cat/37/title/English

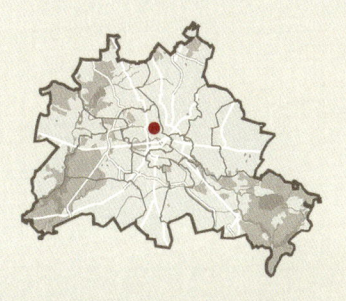

Fighting poverty requires staying power.

Dream figure

tribulations

Step inside and you can hope to come out with a dream figure. This is the realm of the last corsetiere in Berlin to hold the master craftsman's diploma. It's been forty years since the owner, Ursel Rieck, took over the store from her father, who was selling corsets and brassieres at street markets even before the war. His wife was a seamstress, so Ursel—born in the sewing workshop— grew up surrounded by bras and garters, girdles and corsets. She says she has a measuring tape in her eyes. That's what helps her spot each customer's problem zones immediately, and she always has a solution ready. Ursel has passed her exhaustive knowledge of figure-shaping on to her daughter, who now advises the customers just as skillfully as her mother.

Korsett Engelke really ought to be protected as a historical monument. The store is unique, whisking customers into a world that combines solid craftsmanship with a practical and helpful attitude to everyday life, far from the dictates of fashion. It probably didn't look much different fifty years ago. Boxes large and small spill lace and ribbons; the shelves groan under bras in literally every size; and from the workshop comes the whir of the sewing machine as it labors to realize what once seemed to be impossible desires. You can guess at the treasures hidden here, and soon see that the dream of the perfect figure may not necessarily have to remain a dream (→ Ideal).

Location
Korsett Engelke,
Kantstrasse 109, 10627 Berlin

How to get there
U 7 Wilmersdorfer Strasse

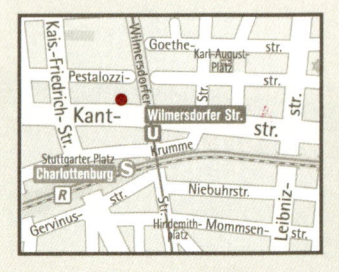

Source

Gabriele Bärtels, "Die Korsett-Königin," *Magazin der Berliner Zeitung*, January 21/22, 2006

Democracy now: dream figures for all!

Expecting

tribulations

"An expectant mother seldom seeks out a doctor at the beginning of her pregnancy, and that is good, since she is not sick," explains an old handbook of helpful hints for mothers-to-be, claiming that it is sufficient to consult a physician four weeks prior to the presumed birth date. Good wishes for the expectant mother had to suffice.

Challenging the medical practice of not letting women make their own decisions, the women's movement historically advocated the right to self-determination. Against the background of having to make a self-determined decision, women today have become the risk managers of their pregnancies. The notion of simply *expecting* a child in the sense of the aforementioned handbook is probably seen today as irresponsible, or at least as imprudent.

Three out of four of all pregnancies today are treated as high-risk pregnancies. The flood of advice handbooks is overwhelming. Should a pregnant woman refrain from coffee and raw-milk cheese? Should she not dye her hair–just to be sure? And so on. Things get complicated with respect to the many prenatal exams. And what about the risk of miscarriage? What if the prenatal test results do not correspond to the statistical norm values? How is a women to make a responsible and self-determined decision whether to continue a pregnancy or have an abortion, on the basis of statistical values and probability and risk calculations? These calculations do not offer any concrete information and are often overwhelming for women. No one wants to return to the past, but in view of the medical and technological options and the growing medicalization of pregnancy and birth, the most important things for pregnant women to have are trust in themselves, encouragement, and support (→ Birthing center).

Location
Charité, Mitte Campus, between Robert-Koch-Platz, Luisen- and Schumannstrasse, 10117 Berlin

How to get there
U 6 Zinnowitzer Strasse,
Bus 240 Robert-Koch-Platz,
Bus 147 Luisenstrasse/Charité

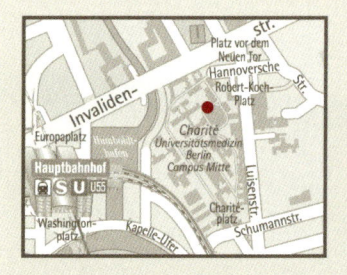

Source
Arbeitskreis Frauengesundheit
www.akf-info.de

To find out more
Silja Samerski, *Die verrechnete Hoffnung. Von der selbstbestimmten Entscheidung durch genetische Beratung*, Münster: Westfälisches Dampfboot, 2002

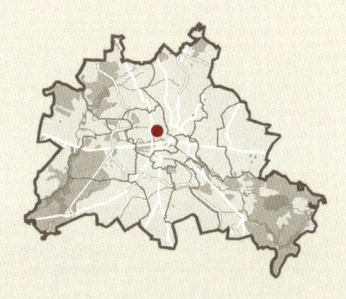

With all the diagnostics, don't forget to expect the best!

Furies

tribulations

The bourgeois public in Berlin was disconcerted and outraged about the behavior of the starving and angry women who stormed the potato stands on April 21, 1847, and went on to plunder the butcher's shop and bakery. The Furies, as the press referred to the desperate women, were from the poorest social classes in the population and they no longer knew how they were to feed their children and families.

As a result of a failed harvest in 1846, prices for groceries, especially potatoes and bread, had exploded to five times the original price. On top of the skyrocketing prices, there was a crisis in the textile industry. This was where women in particular earned their livelihood. Short-time work and unemployment were the outcome. A long harsh winter further worsened the situation for many people. Hardship and misery reached an unprecedented level.

When the potato prices were yet again raised, it was the last straw. By midday on that April 21, the rioting had spread from the Molkenmarkt and Gendarmenmarkt to other markets at Dönhoff Square, Rosenthaler Square and at Oranienburger Gate. The masses of people continued to grow into the evening. Calls for revolution and for the king to step down could be heard. Police and military were out in large numbers. It took them three days to quell the riots.

The women's spontaneous uprising provoked by bitter hardship was like a flash of summer lightning, a prelude to the revolutionary events of March 1848.

Location
Gendarmenmarkt, 10117 Berlin

How to get there
S 1, 2, 25, U 55 Brandenburger Tor, U 2 Stadtmitte, U 6 Französische Strasse

Sources

Cornelia Carstens, Margret Luikenga, and Stephanie von Ow, *Immer den Frauen nach!* ed. Berliner Geschichtswerkstatt e.V., Berlin 1993

Roland Bauer: *Berlin. Illustrierte Chronik bis 1870*, Berlin: Dietz Verlag, 1988

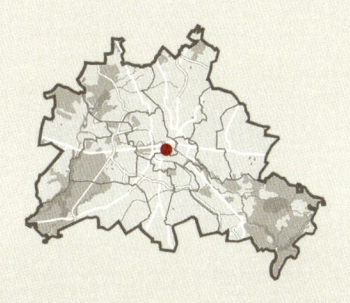

Police bludgeoned the desperate women.

Green Minna

tribulations

Green horse-drawn carriages with air slits, known as Green Minnas, were introduced for prisoner transport by the Berlin police in 1866. Common parlance presumed that in jail the prisoners would be made a *Minna*, or disparaged, feminization being a tried and tested form of humiliation. But women, too, were transported in the Green Minnas. In 1863–64 the Royal Prussian Women's Prison was founded; one of its later prisoners was Rosa Luxemburg (➤ Freedom). Between 1933 and 1945 more than 300 women were imprisoned there before being murdered at Plötzensee (➤ Nuns).

Only 4 percent of prison inmates in Berlin are women. Women behind bars also have to fight for equal treatment. The low number of special women's prisons has led to female prisoners more often than their male counterparts being incarcerated far from their home towns, and thus receiving fewer visits from family members. And women do not profit from the sentence reduction in Berlin, which was introduced due to overcrowded prisons. Offenders who had received fines but were serving time for lack of funds are released after having served half their time. Because there are so few female criminals the women's prisons are not overcrowded and, consequently, there is no sentence reduction.

The fact that women commit less crime has nothing but disadvantages in prison. Prison facilities for women have separate administrations and separate buildings only in Berlin, Hamburg, and Frankfurt am Main. Elsewhere they are nothing but appendages to men's prisons. This means that the women are kept busy with cooking, washing, and mending clothes, and therefore never receive any job training. In the women's prison in Berlin, at least, in addition to jobs in the prison dressmaking shop and the nursery, computer courses are also offered.

Location
Frauenvollzugsanstalt Pankow,
Arkonastrasse 56, 13189 Berlin

How to get there
U 2 Pankow

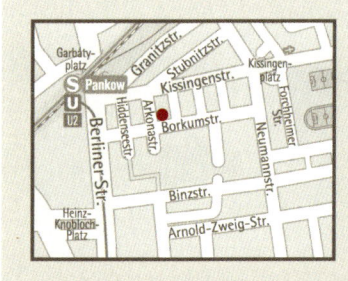

Source
www.luise-berlin.de

To find out more
Commemorative plaque for the Berlin women's prison, Barnimstrasse 10, 10249 Berlin

Equal rights behind bars—not yet reality.

Gypsies

tribulations

Desirous and dangerous, erotic and exotic, full of secrets and spirit, with black hair and smoldering eyes, colorful skirts and clanging jewelry—that is the common cliché of Gypsy women in literature, music, and painting.

"Take the laundry off the clothesline, the Gypsies are coming" was a common saying in the German countryside. Yet people sang of the merry life of a Gypsy and the freedom of the traveling folk. The stereotype is persistent. When they arrive—Roma and Sinti, Kale, Manush, Romanichal, Gitanos or Gypsies—people get agitated. Women in colorful clothing, begging in the streets with their children. Roma women who clean car windshields. Disputes over campsites in Tiergarten or Dreilinden. Discussion about child thieves at Alex. Fear and fascination are two sides of one coin: Yes to the romance of the Gypsies, as long as they aren't disruptive.

The Nazis were categorically suspicious of the Roma and Sinti because they were hard to regulate. In preparation of the 1936 Olympics in Berlin, the "Gypsy plague" was driven from the city and brought to an area in Marzahn that had been used as a sewage field. Being forced to live so close to a cemetery and to sewage was a humiliating violation of religious and cultural taboos. This was the prelude to the annihilation of more than 500,000 Roma and Sinti in so-called family camps in the Auschwitz extermination camp (→ Alex).

Not until 1986 did the Berlin Senate recognize the Marzahn camp as a forced detention camp; now the few survivors can finally receive a pension as victims of political and racial persecution, and only recently was a memorial erected. The Carmen figure from the opera continues to live on in people's minds, but there is no song about the life and suffering of the women in the colorful dresses.

Location
Memorial stone, Marzahn Park Cemetery, Wiesenburger Weg 10, 12681 Berlin

How to get there
S 7 Raoul-Wallenberg-Strasse

Sources
www.minderheiten.org/roma
www.sinti-roma-berlin.de

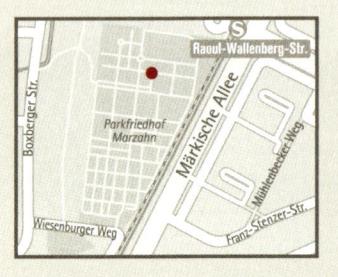

"From May 1936 until our people were liberated by the glorious Soviet Army, hundreds of Sinti suffered in a forced detention camp near this memorial. We honor the victims."

Remembering the sufferings of the Sinti.

Not my bag

tribulations

Going to the bakery is as everyday as the violence that some women suffer within their own four walls. So why not use an everyday item to make an issue of the everyday nature of violence? "Violence? That's not my bag!" It's short and to the point and was printed on thousands of paper bakery bags, so the slogan ended up on the kitchen table along with the breakfast rolls.

First used in Saarbrücken on the occasion of the "No to violence against women" International Action Day on November 25, 2001, the idea was taken up and varied nationwide. More and more anti-violence and women's projects, local women's affairs offices, bakeries, and mayors are participating.

The campaign has been ongoing in Berlin for many years. The district commissioners for women's affairs and equal opportunity, the Berlin Senate, women's organizations, and many Berlin companies spread the word to the public each year on November 25: *"Violence? That's not my bag!"* Companies have sponsored ballpoint pens, lanyard keychains, bags, reusable hand warmers, radiator keys, or shopping cart chips featuring the slogan.

Violence against women is an intractable problem. The first battered women's shelter in Germany was started about thirty years ago in Berlin. The women's movement had to fight a long battle to overcome the resistance. Women's shelters and safe apartments help women to escape violence, but it's just as important to prevent it. Domestic violence is a crime, and is finally being investigated and prosecuted as such by police and the courts. Nevertheless, many women and their children continue to feel humiliated and threatened for their lives in their own homes (→ Honor).

Location
Memorial stone for Hatun Sürücü,
Oberlandgarten 1
at Oberlandstrasse, 12099 Berlin

How to get there
S 41, 42, 46, 47,
U 8 Hermannstrasse,
Bus 246 Oberlandgarten

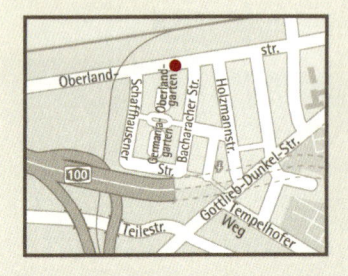

Source
Lisa Glahn, *Frauen im Aufbruch. 20 Jahre Geschichte und Gegenwart Autonomer Frauenhäuser*, Münster: Unrast Verlag, 1998

To find out more
www.big-koordinierung.de

For a home without violence

Out, out, out ...

tribulations

Theories of Germany's *Sonderweg*, its separate path to modernization, certainly inspire the great historical models of German scholars. Often lost in the process, unfortunately, is a small detail: the modest but tenacious attempts, along the final steps of the unstoppable path to democracy, to keep women out of the defined scope of the citizen, with its guaranteed right to participate in democratic events. How long did the German nobility and bourgeoisie, German nature and German culture, and—lest we forget—German police successfully ward off all things democratic and thus womanish! Where once the feeble mind of the woman was wholeheartedly asserted and joyously welcomed, the right to vote and femininity were declared mutually exclusive, and after attempts to the contrary the male pride of Nazism was exalted in all its greatness, the only doubt the young German democracy could allow was poetic. "On her own the woman in parliament seems like a flower, but en masse like weeds," a knowledgeable agrarian politician dared to assert as late as the 1950s. To no avail. The four mothers of the Basic Law finally brought an end to the phantom of the special essence of femaleness (➛ **Mothers**). Men and women shall have equal rights. Period. That's it. One third of Germany's parliament are weeds? Don't worry—you can't get rid of weeds! Even Claire Waldoff—known as a ➛ **Berlin flower**, meaning she put down roots in Berlin—knew that, as she sang at the top of her lungs, "Get the men out, out, out of parliament!" If only people had listened to her earlier.

Location
Reichstag, Platz der Republik 1, 10557 Berlin

How to get there
S 1, 2, 25, U 55 Brandenburger Tor

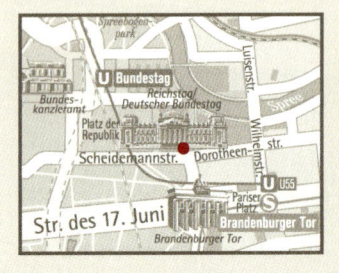

Source
http://de.wikipedia.org/wiki/
 Michael_Horlacher

To find out more
Claudia von Gélieu, *Vom Politik-verbot ins Kanzleramt. Ein hürdenreicher Weg für Frauen*, Berlin: Lehmanns Media, 2008

Why not? Out means out!

Outside

tribulations

No place exists without an outside around it. An *outside*, where all that is displaced and singled out is sent. A place such as Ravensbrück.

As a place, Ravensbrück is a small village in the middle of an idyllic lake district north of Berlin. As an *outside*, Ravensbrück was the women's concentration camp established in 1939. An *outside* for women who according to the Nazi ideology of racial purity were to be exterminated. And for women who resisted Nazi ideology and believed in humane ideals. A horrific *outside* of the "Aryan national community."

For the roughly 132,000 women and children, 20,000 men, and 1,000 female adolescents incarcerated there, Ravensbrück was not an *outside* but a place of suffering, where they struggled to survive, where tens of thousands died from starvation, disease, torture, and medical experimentation.

For the Siemens & Halske company and for the companies in forty other satellite camps, Ravensbrück was not an *outside*, but a lucrative production site with cheap labor.

Since 1945 Ravensbrück has been a place of memory. And an *outside* of memory. A place to remember heroic communist women. An *outside* to remember politically and socially undesirable victims. A place for commemoration. An *outside* in the memory of the region. A place for deserted buildings and using concentration camp buildings as barracks. When Germany was just reunited it was the place where a supermarket was planned, but also a place for reflection and reconstructing memories. An *outside* in the hierarchy of the memories. No place as the "concentration camp of the Reich capital," as Sachsenhausen has recently been called. A place of women indeed, both a place and *outside* at the same time.

Location
Topographie des Terrors,
Niederkirchnerstrasse 8,
10117 Berlin

How to get there
S-Bahn and U-Bahn,
Bus 200 Potsdamer Platz,
S 1, 2, 25 Anhalter Bahnhof

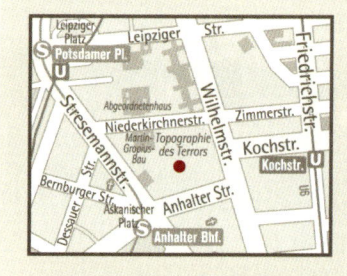

To find out more

www.topographie.de

Mahn- und Gedenkstätte Ravensbrück, Stiftung Brandenburgische Gedenkstätten, Strasse der Nationen, 16798 Fürstenberg

www.ravensbrueck.de

"Die Frauen von Ravensbrück. Das Videoarchiv," Loretta Walz, biographical documentaries, Düsseldorf 2009

The place of the perpetrators, in the midst of the national community

Red-light *tribulations*

For some, it is the latest notion of marketing oneself in the name of self-determination; for others, it is a slave market of misery and splendor. Splendor in the eyes of those who skim profit from the estimated €15 billion taken in annually—in Germany alone. Splendor in the eyes of the johns who find a willing helper for every wish, no matter where or how. And splendor in the imagination of artists, who in the twilight of a brothel invoke a grandiose counterworld to bourgeois boredom. And the misery? Does the double standard still exist that forced unlucky women to sell their bodies, while the young men sought their sexual initiation with the prostitutes and practiced the proper conduct of a man? Didn't the free market do magic by turning the enslaved whore into a provider of sexual services that satisfies the demands of the market?

In times of globalization and self-reliance, every woman is the architect of her own fate. Only embarrassing die-hards speak of the misery stalking behind the young female drug addicts, the survivors of sexual abuse, the women trafficked more or less against their will in international brothels (→ **Working girls**). Millions of johns can't be wrong, so you gladly give in to the illusion in lecture halls and political circles that prostitution is an act of self-determination and moral liberation. But what does sex without an equal partner do to the men who buy it, the people who deliver it, and the women who seek egalitarian relationships?

Red is the color of love. Red lights point the way to the brothels. It is a cynical theory of color that boasts of love, lust, and the fullness of life, where exploitation, business, and male megalomaniacal dreams are celebrated.

Location
Historic traffic light (traffic tower) at Potsdamer Platz, 10785 Berlin

How to get there
S-Bahn and U-Bahn,
Bus 200 Potsdamer Platz

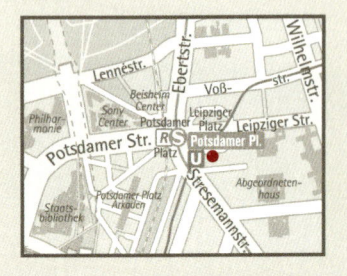

189

Lust and profit for johns and pimps

Soup-kitchen Lina

tribulations

Opening day kept being postponed. What the men couldn't do wouldn't get done in three days by a woman—at least that's what the head of the committee for public soup kitchens said. But Lina Morgenstern was energetic, indefatigable, and pragmatic through and through; and she did it. On July 4, 1866, she opened the first Berlin public soup kitchen on a trial basis.

It was successful, and fifteen other kitchens followed. Known as Soup-kitchen Lina, Lina Morgenstern pit herself against the most dire need, but her involvement went much further than that. Raised in a well-off Jewish family, on her eighteenth birthday she founded the *Pfennigverein*, the penny club, to provide poor schoolchildren with clothing, books, and school supplies. She wrote children's books to feed her family of five children, published articles on questions of child-rearing, and founded eight daycare centers and a school for kindergarten teachers. She publicly denounced prostitution and founded an organization to help young women get out of it (→ Working girls).

Her understanding of charity came from her great intuition regarding the problems and everyday concerns of women. She didn't want merely to provide practical assistance, but also to actively oppose the fateful practice of gender tutelage by men. She published 250 biographies of women, thereby commemorating social and political traditions. She didn't give a hoot about the divisions between the bourgeois, radical, and socialist women's movements, and organized Germany's first international women's congress together with Minna Cauer in September 1896 in Berlin. As a passionate pacifist, she fought the disastrous ways of militarism and chauvinism and thus became a pioneer of peace activism.

Location
Grave at the Weissensee Jewish Cemetery, Herbert-Baum-Strasse 45, 13088 Berlin

How to get there
Tram M 4, M 13 Antonplatz or Albertinenstrasse

Sources
Heinz Knobloch, *Die Suppenlina. Wiederbelebung einer Menschenfreundin*, Berlin 1997

www.luise-berlin.de/bms/bmstxt97/9712prod.htm

Beate Neubauer and Claudia von Gélieu, *Kurfürstin, Köchin, Karrierefrau*, Berlin 2005

To find out more

Memorial plaque at Linienstrasse 47, 10119 Berlin

Lina-Morgenstern-Oberschule, Gneisenaustrasse 7, 10961 Berlin

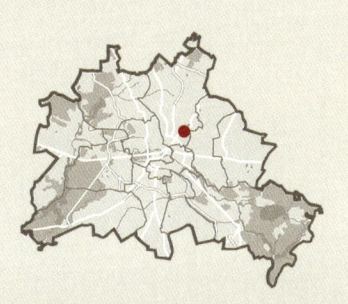

Indefatigable in her fight for justice and peace

The Wall

tribulations

For some it was the Antifascist Protective Wall, for others it was the Iron Curtain. It divided the city of Berlin from August 13, 1961, until November 9, 1989, and separated families and friends. It was a martially controlled and armed border and cost many refugees their lives.

It is the reason why perceptions in East and West differ. Images and ideas on each side about the other side took on a life of their own. When women from East and West encountered each other for the first time after the fall of the Wall, they initially saw only the distorted images in their heads. There were childless "women's libbers" who fought against men and who were politically correct enough to add the female ending to every profession when referring to women, and beside them the species of the "housewife" that had become foreign to them—on the one side. And on the other side were the hardworking, employed East German women who were totally blind to the male domination of society, and in their shadow the clueless "East mommy." This all had to do with reality to the extent that that the quota of employed women in the East was high, whereas the level in the West was far lower. And that there was a broad-based women's movement in the West, whereas in the East there was state-sanctioned equality. Although the life stories and lifestyles were and are very different, the political ideas in terms of women's issues quickly came together: More women in leadership positions, securing an independent livelihood, fighting violence against women, providing adequate childcare, and self-determined pregnancy(→ Cyanide) are on the agenda throughout the country. If women had been in charge of German-German unification, we would be a lot farther along.

Location
Watchtower Monument at the Spandau shipping canal (watchtower of the former command post at Kieler Eck), Kieler Strasse 2, 10115 Berlin

How to get there
U 6 Naturkundemuseum or Schwartzkopffstrasse

To find out more

www.berliner-mauerdokumenta
 tionszentrum.de

www.eastsidegallery.com

A country without a wall is like a fish without a bicycle.

Working girls

tribulations

"Berlin women are not servants," is what people said around 1870. Instead, Berlin housewives would find a young girl from the countryside or the provinces: inexperienced, modest, and used to meager earnings and hard work.

When Berlin became the capital of the empire and started growing by leaps and bounds, young women came to Berlin, especially from the eastern provinces, to escape rural life as a farmgirl—up to 40,000 each year. This left its mark on the city in the architecture of the period. Residences had separate servants' entrances, tiny maids' rooms, and the notorious crawlspace above a suspended ceiling that served as the girls' sleeping quarters; this all bears witness to the disappearance of the willing hands of servants within the bourgeois household. Hard work, limited free time, poor food, little sleep, and being at the mercy of the moods of the lady of the house and often the desires of the master—as a result, there was much fluctuation in the maids' positions. Employers would note their behavior and industriousness in the servants' log, thereby determining their future employment chances. Having their own family seemed a desirable destiny, even if poverty and large families were the rule.

When the naïve rural girls arrived at the train station, women were often waiting to pick them up and lure them into prostitution (→ **Soup-kitchen Lina**). Double standards and the girls' helplessness brought flourishing business for pimps (→ **Red-light**).

Today, the currency differential between Germany and Eastern Europe again provides Berlin with inexpensive housecleaning personnel. Many of them work illegally or for very low wages and most have no insurance coverage. But at least most of them can close the door when they finish work and return to their own apartments.

Location
Heimatmuseum Pankow,
Heynstrasse 8, 13187 Berlin

How to get there
U 2, S 2, 8 Pankow,
Bus 250 Görschstrasse

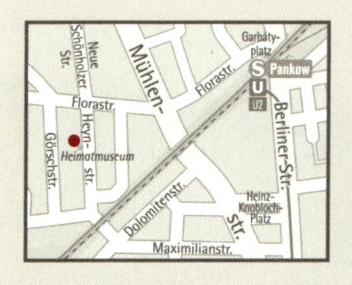

Sources

Dietlinde Peters, "Drei schlesische Dienstmädchen in Berlin," in *"Wach auf, mein Herz, und denke." Zur Geschichte der Beziehungen zwischen Schlesien und Berlin-Brandenburg* (exhibition catalogue), Berlin/Opole 1995

www.expolis.de

At your service around the clock

oases

artemis

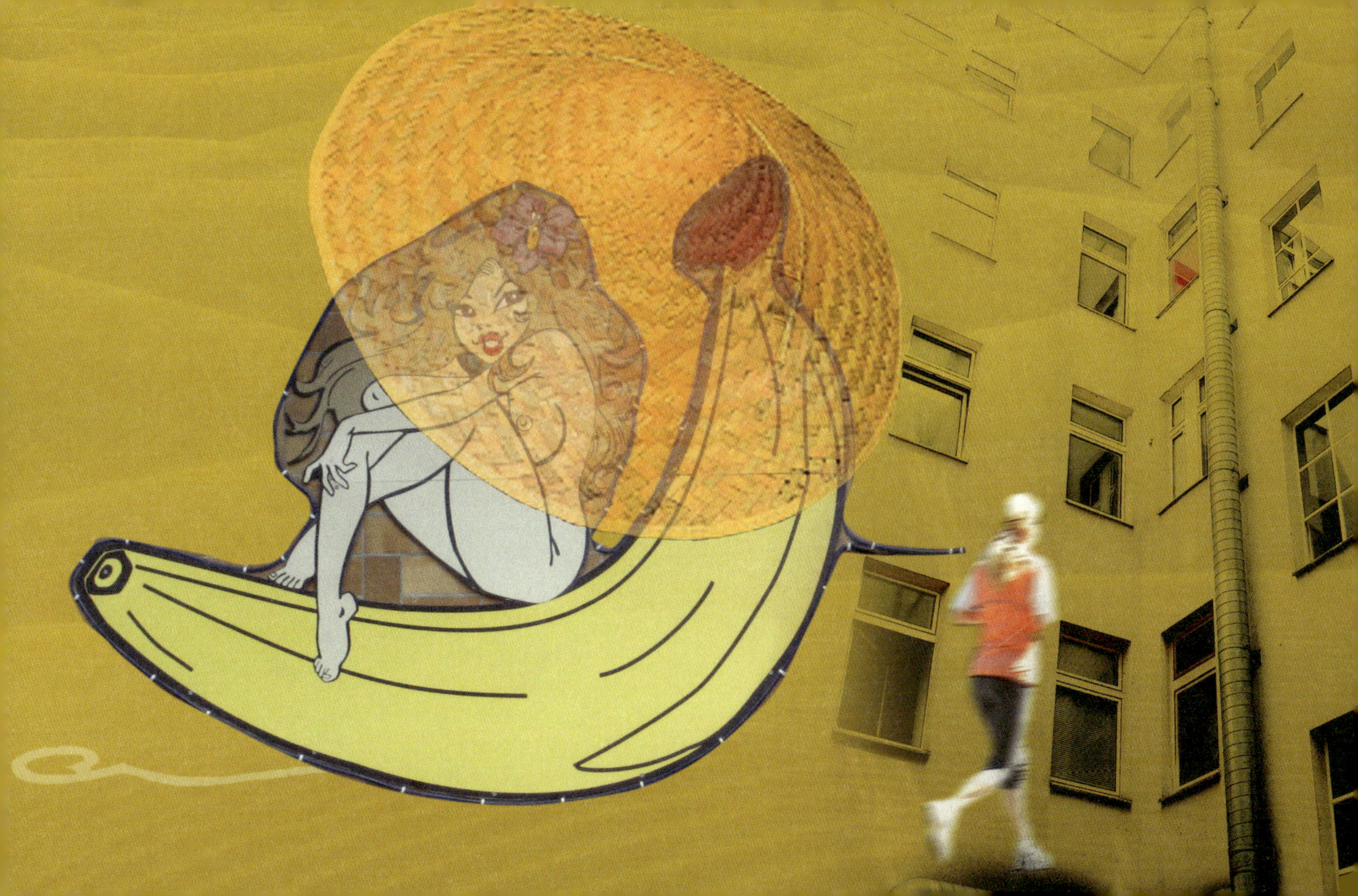

Artemisia

oases

When the women who started Berlin's first hotel for women more than 20 years ago initiated a radio appeal asking for suggestions for a name, they surprisingly received a suggestion that meandered clear through women's history (➤ Clio).

Artemisia, known as common wormwood and mugwort, is highly esteemed in traditional gynecology because of its relaxing effect. The plant was dedicated to the Goddess Artemis, Isis, Diana, and the Virgin Mary (➤ Maiden). In other words, an herb of women, and a pioneer plant as well, which—mother of all plants—is the first to colonize previously uncolonized land, starting ecological succession.

This was the perfect name for Artemisia Gentileschi (1597–1653), who at the height of the Renaissance fought to be the first woman to study at the art academy in Rome. She became famous with her painting *Judith Slaying Holofernes*, also because she dared to accuse the man who had raped her in her father's studio. Like her male colleagues, she used images from the Bible and antiquity for her artistic expression, but she was the first woman to express her pain, rage, and strength of self-assertion in her work. She certainly knew nothing about the Carian princess Artemisia, who had one of the Seven Wonders of the Ancient World built: The Mausoleum of Halicarnassos, in present-day Bodrum, was completed in the 4th century BCE. It honored her husband-brother King Mausolus, after whose death Artemisia ruled over Caria and Rhodes.

An oasis to feel good in and at the same time a place for art. The Artemisia women's hotel takes up this intertwined tradition. Others have followed the example of this hotel in Berlin. Now there are many places where women traveling alone can enjoy women-friendly accommodations as a matter of course.

Location
Herb garden, Naturschutzstation Malchow e.V., Dorfstrasse 35, 13051 Berlin

How to get there
Bus 154 und 259 Malchow / Dorfstrasse

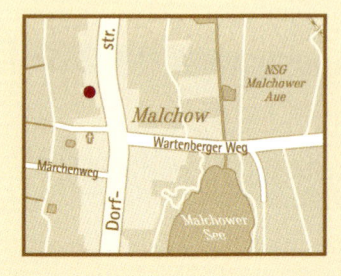

Source
www.frauenhotel-berlin.de

To find out more
Susan Vreeland, *The Passion of Artemisia*, New York: Penguin, 2002

Artemisia: An herb for goddess and commoner alike

Beguines

oases

A look at the map is overwhelming: settlements of the Beguines were established in the Middle Ages in very close proximity to one another in southwestern Germany and throughout all of the German lands. Berlin was no exception. Women worked, lived, and managed their communities together—an idea that has never been totally lost, even if urban planners, architects, and ministries of housing in modern times have tended instead to think in nuclear family terms in designing living schemes. Whether béguinage or convent, or the Ottilie von Hansemann House built by architect Emilie Winkelmann in the early 20th century for the first female students, or the *Hexenhaus* (Witches' House) squatted by women in the 1980s—women continue to create ways to live together according to their own plan.

Since 2007 Berlin has once again had a béguinage. After fifteen years of hard work, a new upscale building was erected in the middle of Kreuzberg, offering more than fifty women space to live both independently and in community. A stroke of luck for the neighborhood and an impetus for new projects. After all, there are 600,000 single women in Berlin, and their numbers are growing steadily.

Location
BeginenWerk,
Erkelenzdamm 51–57,
10999 Berlin

How to get there
U 8 Kottbusser Tor

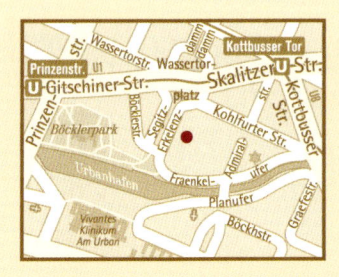

To find out more

www.beginenwerk.de
www.berlin.de/ba-charlottenburg-
  wilmersdorf/bezirk/lexikon/
  hansemann-haus.html

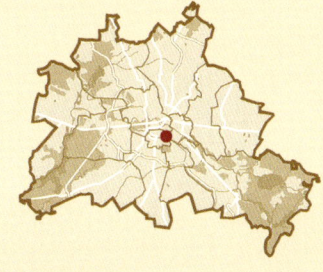

Boulette and mocca faux

oases

Berlin is famous for a lot of things, but not its cuisine. Berlin food tends to be heavy: *Buletten* (like big, flat meatballs), bockwurst, and its own variety of cured pork knuckle—even though Berlin went through numerous phases of French influence over the centuries! The French part is apparent when reading any menu: Filet and *Kotelet*t (cutlet), ragout and bouillon, *Pastete* (pastry) and omelette, dessert, and so on. Even the typically Berliner *Bulette* comes from the French *boule* (ball) and its diminutive *boulette*. In 1685, Elector Friedrich Wilhelm of Brandenburg offered refuge to the Huguenots, who were being persecuted in France. By the late 17th century, one in five Berliners was a religious refugee. The Huguenots brought more than just tobacco, asparagus, cauliflower, eggplant, artichokes, and beans with them; they also brought refined manners, table etiquette, and good eating habits (➤ Fisimatenten). Opinions diverge on how lastingly eating habits actually improved. The sophistication suffered a bit with the new culinary influences of fast food and take out.

Multicultural Berlin has a very varied cuisine. Fusion is the order of the day, the more or less successful mixture of different ethnic influences.

But nowadays Berliners tend to cook at home less and eat in restaurants more. The everyday, unpaid job of cooking at home is generally done by women. The well-paid, famous chefs are usually men. But women are catching up. Some, like Sarah Wiener, who runs three Berlin restaurants, belong to the category of celebrity chef. Deserving its bad reputation, however, at the bottom of Berlin's coffee culture scale, is its coffee substitute, called *Muckefuck*. A malapropism of the French *mocca faux*, or false coffee, it tells the inglorious story of deprivation and poverty.

Location
Das Speisezimmer,
Chausseestrasse 8, 10115 Berlin

How to get there
U 6 Oranienburger Tor, Bus 240
Torstrasse / Oranienburger Strasse

Sources
Kulturamt Pankow (ed.), *Von märkischer Derbheit zu französischem Flair*, Berlin 2000

Cyril Buffet, *Fisimatenten. Franzosen in Berlin*, ed. Ausländerbeauftragte des Berliner Senats, Berlin 2004

To find out more
Arnt Cobbers, *Berlin-Mitte. Der aufregendste Bezirk: Zwischen Tradition und Szene*, Berlin: Jaron Verlag, 2005

An end to deprivation: Latté replaces mocca faux

Chocolate

oases

"I don't want chocolate, I want the whole factory!" That might have been the secret motto of women from the feminist and alternative scene who squatted an abandoned chocolate factory, or *Schokofabrik*, in the heart of Kreuzberg in 1981. Within weeks in the winter of 1980–81, more than a hundred buildings in Berlin were squatted to preserve usable housing and protest the widespread demolition and new construction.

But the Schokofabrik women had more in mind. They dreamed of a neighborhood center where women could freely develop and live their ideas of politics, recreation, art, education, and athletics. Schwarze Schokolade, a group of women artists, used the openness of the unmodernized factory lofts for experimental projects. In the Schokoschnute daycare center, girls and boys could grow up free of role constraints. The first hamam (Turkish bathhouse) in Berlin was opened, despite financial and architectural obstacles. Green and glass roofs and composting toilets were among the experiments in ecological construction. Visitors from all over Europe were amazed at the 21,000 sq. feet of space designed by and for women. Dance parties from tango to techno delighted thousands and brought in money to work on the Schokocafé, the sports floors, the educational work including literacy and German classes, counseling options such as the women's crisis telephone, and work with girls. Countless women came with ideas and energy to bring the space to life. Many supporters were found within the neighborhood, urban development offices, and the Berlin Senate. In 2004, the women—and many donors—bought the Schokofabrik building to secure the project's future.

Women's spaces are still rare. The Schoko women let their dreams grow and come true. Almost without chocolate—and almost without men.

Location
Frauenzentrum
Schokoladenfabrik e.V.,
Mariannenstrasse 6,
10997 Berlin

How to get there
U 1 Görlitzer Bahnhof

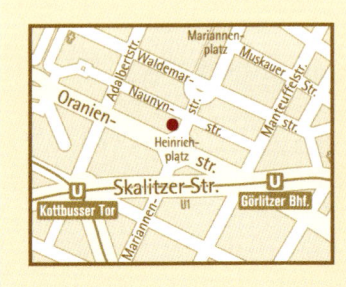

To find out more
www.schokofabrik.de

They have chocolate too—in Café Marianne.

Girls move

oases

Commuter rail line S75 ends at Wartenberg station. Right there, amid buildings eleven stories high, there is a former *Fresswürfel*, or "food cube," a school cafeteria building, as was common in housing projects in East Germany. The schools are gone now, and the "food cube" was no longer in use.

That was a great opportunity for Pia Olymp, a girls' sports center, of which there are very few in Berlin. Their aim is to get girls excited about sports, especially girls around puberty. That is when many girls stop doing sports even if they were athletic as a kid, either because they no longer like the club structures, or they have other interests, or they think sports are uncool. And sometimes they refocus their energy and interests around their clique or boyfriend. But sports and exercise are very helpful in overcoming the numerous pitfalls of growing up, dealing with the dramatic changes in one's body, and developing an independent, self-assured identity as a woman. There are many reasons to encourage young women to continue coming out to the athletic fields.

Together with skilled tradeswomen from Baufachfrau Berlin in Weissensee, girls from Pia Olymp developed ideas for mobile sports activities in the empty lots in the neighborhood. Sports equipment, such as for skating, was invented and built. The Rolling Golfer is a real hit. It is a suitcase with a portable miniature golf game that can be set up almost anywhere—in a park, an office, a senior citizens' home. The Golfer can be borrowed from the girls' sports center, other recreation centers, or the IN VIA women's project in Karlshorst. In 2006 Pia Olymp's "girls move" project won third prize in the Golden Göre ("Golden Imp") competition, the highest award of the German Children's Relief Organization (DKHW) (→ **Berlin air**).

Location
Mädchensportzentrum Pia Olymp,
Am Berl 25, 13051 Berlin

How to get there
S 75 Wartenberg

To find out more

www.maedchensportzentrum-pia-olymp.de
Girls' sports center of the Verein für Sport und Jugendsozialarbeit in Neukölln, www.neukoelln-jugend.de/wildehuette/

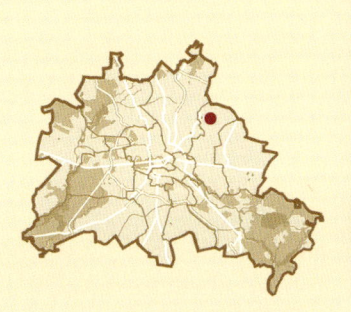

Watch out Olympics: Pia girls are on the move

Out in the boondocks

oases

When something is "out in the boondocks" Berliners say it is *janz weit draussen*—or *JWD* for short. Since time immemorial that is where women in Berlin hope to escape the draining, gray rat race of the city. It could be Wannsee at the city's edge or Usedom, Berliners' famous bathtub at the Baltic Sea, or as far as La Gomera, one of the Canary Islands, where West Berliners who were tired of coal heating tried to get away from the long dismal winters.

After the Wall came down, West Berlin got a present; it was called surroundings, environs! And it could be reached by commuter rail (S-Bahn). A wealth of hiking groups and tour suggestions and restaurant or event tips shot up out of nowhere, to help the capital's women discover these environs.

In addition to forests, lakes, and beaches, when you are jwd there are also exciting places to visit where women were at work. Please feel free to explore!

Location
Müggelsee, Licht- und Luftbad,
Fürstenwalder Damm,
12589 Berlin

How to get there
S 3 Friedrichshagen, then Tram 61
Licht- und Luftbad Müggelsee

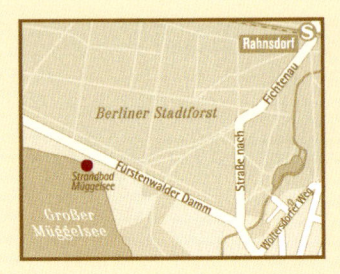

Don't forget to pack your bathing suits …

Out in the boondocks *oases*

To find out more

Wiepersdorf Palace
Summer residence and final resting place of Bettina von Arnim (1785–1859) (➤ Book of the Poor), since 2006 a center for artists with artist-in-residence fellowships.
Bettina-von-Arnim-Strasse 13, 14913 Wiepersdorf,
www.schloss-wiepersdorf.de

Schloss Bad Freienwalde
Palace and residence of Friederike Luise of Hesse-Darmstadt (1751–1805), widow of Friedrich Wilhelm II (1744–1797).
Rathenaustrasse 3,
16259 Bad Freienwalde

Mosigkau Palace
Noble ladies' convent (1780–1945), founded as a social welfare facility for unmarried aristocratic women in the year that Princess Anna Wilhelmine (1715–1780) died, in accordance with her decree. It was maintained until the end of World War II (parts are a museum today).
Knobelsdorffallee 2/3,
06847 Dessau-Mosigkau

Oranienburg Palace
Luise Henriette, Princess of Orange (1627–1667),
wife of the Great Elector Friedrich Wilhelm (1620–1688),
Schlossplatz 2, 16515 Oranienburg

Penzlin
Witch's dungeon; witch burnings took place here until 1703.
Museum Alte Burg,
Warener Chaussee 55 a,
17217 Penzlin

Pfaueninsel (Peacock Island)
World Heritage Site, small romantic castle, referred to at the time as a Roman manor house, greatly influenced by "Beautiful Wilhelmine" (born Wilhelmine Encke or Enke, 1753–1820), 1796 became Countess of Lichtenau, royal mistress of Friedrich Wilhelm II (1744–1797).
Pfaueninselchaussee 1,
14109 Berlin

Palace theater in the New Palace in Potsdam
Workplace of dancer Barberina Campanini (1721–1799), also called the Flying Goddess by her admirers, including Friedrich II.
Am Neuen Palais, 14469 Potsdam

Rheinsberg
Setting for Kurt Tucholsky's (1890–1935) novel Rheinsberg. *Ein Bilderbuch für Verliebte* (Rheinsberg: A Picture Book for Lovers), in which he memorializes the modern, self-assured woman of the 1920s
(➤ Girls from the office).
www.rheinsberg.de

Fashion Museum, Meyenburg Palace

Collection of Josefine Edle von Krepl, 1900–1970, exhibition, café and antique fashion store, where historic originals are for sale at affordable prices (20th-century clothing, hats, handbags, and many accessories). Josefine Edle von Krepl has one of the largest private fashion collections in the world. She started collected clothing and accessories from the past in East Germany, sometimes saving them from being discarded. In the—now very classy—neighborhood around Boxhagener Square in Friedrichshain she ran a very popular boutique in the 1980s, where she sold fashions she designed and tailored herself. Her extravagant designs with the small "Josefine" label in the collar were added to the collection of the German Historical Museum in 1997.
www.modemuseum-schlossmeyenburg.de

Rheinsberg Castle—old walls, new women

Paradise

oases

Berlin is green. Around 2,500 parks and green spaces offer areas for exercise and recreation for people and pets. There are also 76,165 allotment gardens (like community garden lots with cottages on them) where a lucky subspecies of Berliners can live out the eternal dream of paradise. On more than 7,700 acres, allotment holders plant and harvest; dig, weed and water; sunbathe; argue and celebrate; and of course barbecue, barbecue, barbecue. Allotment gardens reduce noise and dust, lower the urban building density, and placate the need to return to the land to a degree compatible with city life (➤ **Berlin air**).

These gardens emerged during industrialization to give working-class families a chance to enhance their living standard despite their meager wages. The first "colonies" of allotment gardens in Berlin were in the Rehberge park in the working-class district of Wedding.

After the war, many cottages were used as full-time residences. This became increasingly frowned upon as real estate prices started to climb, and with the fall of the Berlin Wall it became a serious problem, since gardens in former East Berlin had previously been spared the pressure to sell the land. Now the colonies are considered ecological reserves and only rarely sacrificed, such as to build an autobahn extension.

In large housing projects such as Marzahn-Hellersdorf (➤ **Prefab high-rise**), tenants were allowed to convert empty lots into small gardens to improve their quality of life. Pleasure in gardening is shared among many ethnic groups. In intercultural gardens such as the Wuhlegarten, gardening friends from eleven countries work their bit of land (➤ **Multiculti**). When the barbecue fanatics start talking shop around the grill and recipes are traded in the kitchen, then paradise is within reach.

Location
"Berg und Tal" allotment garden colony, can be seen from S-Bahnhof Greifswalder Strasse, 10407 Berlin

How to get there
S 8, 41, 42,
Tram M 4 Greifswalder Strasse

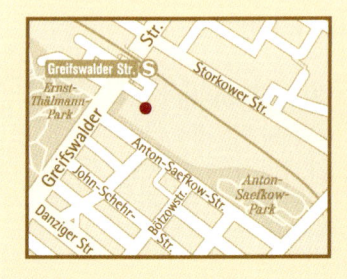

Source

www.stadtentwicklung.berlin.de/
 umwelt/stadtgruen/kleingaerten/

Between the barbecue and the hedge the world is still in order.

Pietà

oases

After her son was killed in World War I, the mourning artist Käthe Kollwitz created a sculpture reminiscent of the Christian Pietà: the mother with her dead son on her lap. Almost eighty years later, the small figure was enlarged many times and placed at the center of the newly erected memorial of the Federal Republic of Germany at the Neue Wache (New Guardhouse) on the Unter den Linden boulevard.

This marked the pinnacle of the bitter debate on the new national image of united Germany. Here, where victims of war and tyranny were to be officially commemorated, where the dispute was raging whether it was permissible to remember murdered Jews and fallen SS soldiers together, where the naming of individual groups of victims was attacked as a kind of "human selection," this was precisely the site where the Christian motif of the Virgin Mary mourning the death of her son was to be the main symbolic message? Would Jewish victims be able to identify with this image? How did this express the suffering of the millions of murdered, starved, exiled, expelled, and raped women and girls? The Pietà as the central image of national commemoration masks the genocide and the suffering of women. It portrays war as an encounter of courageous warriors in open battles. But the young German fighter was neither the only nor the real victim. He killed the elderly, fathers and sons; he raped mothers and daughters. He brought the murdering to villages, churches, and synagogues throughout Europe, to ditches, ghettos, and gas chambers. Under what rubble and in which mass grave does his mother lie? The intimate image of a mourning mother and fallen son tells an inappropriately sentimental story of war and crimes of violence.

Location
Neue Wache,
Unter den Linden 4,
10117 Berlin

How to get there
Bus 100, 200 Staatsoper

To find out more

Places in Berlin that commemorate Käthe Kollwitz: Kollwitzplatz and Kollwitzstrasse in Prenzlauer Berg, Käthe Kollwitz Museum, Fasanenstrasse 24, 10719 Berlin

Silke Wenk, "Die Mutter in der Mitte Berlins. Strategien der Rekonstruktion eines Hauptstadtzentrums," in Gisela Ecker (ed.), *Kein Land in Sicht. Heimat – weiblich?* Munich: Wilhelm Fink, 1997

Who is commemorated? Who is not?

Prefab high-rise

oases

The prefabricated concrete slab construction style, known as *Platte*, has become a synonym for the typical architecture and housing style in East Germany, although its beginnings go back to the 1920s. The first German prefab housing project was unveiled in 1927 in Berlin-Lichtenberg. And the New Frankfurt residential housing program that was completed in the early 1930s was built in part using *Platte* construction.

East Germany first decided to use this style of housing in the mid-1950s. The motto then was: faster, cheaper, better. Industrial construction promised high-speed building, low costs, and higher quality of life. Industrially produced concrete slabs were built into residential blocks on a massive scale and almost everyone who received one of these new apartments felt lucky. *Einzug ins Paradies* (Entering Paradise) was the name of an East German television series (1985) that illustrated the ups and downs in the lives of the new residents of an eleven-story prefab high-rise. In West Berlin as well, major residential projects built largely using industrial construction methods (prefab and slab construction) sprung up, such as Gropiusstadt in the south or Märkisches Viertel in the north.

On both sides of the city, people complain today about the monotony of the architecture (➔ Run-of-the-mill) and the tiny kitchens in all these buildings (although they were modeled after the "Frankfurt kitchen," state-of-the-art at the time). The advantages of such housing projects are now also being mentioned: spacious open and planted areas, safer for children through lack of traffic, less industry-related environmental pollution, pedestrian-oriented design of the centers. Efforts are being made to revive the *Platte* with gardens, terraces, and artistic experiments.

Location
Splanemann-Siedlung,
Sewanstrasse/Splanemannstrasse,
10319 Berlin

How to get there
U 5 Tierpark

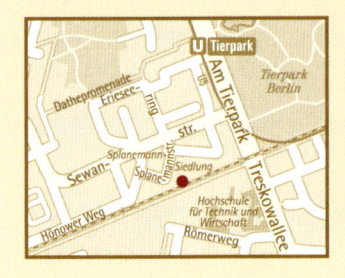

To find out more

Pension 11. Himmel – Accommodations in the Marzahn *Platte*, Tel.: +49 (30) 93772052

Museum apartment Hellersdorfer Strasse 179, 12627 Berlin, Authentically furnished 3-room, prefab slab construction, Tours on Sundays from 2 to 4 pm, or call for arrangements: +49 (151) 16 11 44 40

Prefabs also come in upscale.

Prima donna

oases

Typesetting machines as big as wardrobes, disks in pizza-box format, and a light table with a scissors and glue–that is how the first postmodern women's magazine (as the proud makers called it) was produced in night shifts, when they could use the rooms for free. What today appears technically archaic was an intellectually ambitious project. The *Primadonna*, smart and beautiful, postmodern but certainly not post-feminist, danced its way out of the heads–and hands–of the women who created it in the final years of West Berlin before the Wall fell. *Primadonna* was ironic, but always meant seriously, of course feminist and yet arrogant, a playground for ambitious spirits who were open to avant-garde experiments, and a sociocultural and journalistic challenge for the editorial department. "Drei Dinge braucht die Inge" (Ms. Ings needs three things) was the name of a column–what more could a woman need? The patriarchy was lampooned, but not libeled. Making a newspaper, as the primordial scene of intellectual consciousness-raising, led the women, dramas, and discourses to incredible heights.

Due to internal strife and a disturbing lack of funds, the *Primadonna* came to an end at the same time as the Wall did. It shared the same fate as many "in" magazines of the women's movement. For a few years it was the place for women of a feminist generation to share ideas, developing them further and then going their own ways. Other magazines followed, such as *Blau* (Blue) and *Ypsilon* (Y)–nowadays there are many Internet magazines. Their sisters who became better established, such as *Emma*, *Blattgold*, and *Aviva*, continue to offer reliable information and reports. This hasn't affected the charm of the intellectual dreams of each new generation of free-floating feminists.

Location
The former workshop of the Gegensatz printers in Kreuzberg, Eisenbahnstrasse 4, 10997 Berlin

How to get there
U 1 Schlesisches Tor or Görlitzer Bahnhof, Bus 140 Wrangelstrasse

To find out more
FFBIZ Women's Research, Education, and Information Center, Eldenaerstrasse 35 III, 10247 Berlin

Lots of room for feminist flights of fancy

Run, Lola, Run!

oases

How to get 100,000 marks in twenty minutes—it isn't easy, so Lola runs and runs to save her friend's life. What seems so dramatic in a movie is far less spectacular in real life, but it exists. Berlin women and girls run and jog and walk like mad! The huge Women's Run, for instance, sponsored each May by Avon Running, now attracts some 15,000 runners and walkers to the Tiergarten Park each year (➤ **Amazon**).

Berlin with its many parks offers ideal conditions to run in almost every district. In view of the limited free time that most women have, it's all the more important to have a park or green space to run in right near the house door. Safety and protection from unleashed dogs (➤ **Dogs**) help determine whether running is pleasurable or not, or whether a woman goes running at all. In many parks there is still a lot to be done with regard to lighting, safety, and pet control. One place that is perfect for running in every respect is the Britz Garden.

Running, like many things in life, is a matter of disposition. Some run alone, some with music; others prefer a group to chat with or to overcome their lack of will power.

Even if nature gave people all they need to go running, the athletic clothing industry discovered some room for—even gender-specific—improvement. If you have short legs, broad hips, or a short torso, then you fit into some companies' special "women's line." But don't worry: they won't let anyone go naked or barefoot, and there are clothing and shoes for all. Anyway, Lola has no time to waste mulling over that. She ran with what she had on, and guess what: it worked.

Location
Britzer Garten,
Mohriner Allee 142, 12347 Berlin

How to get there
Bus 181 Rotkopfweg

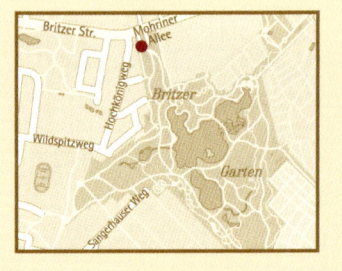

To find out more

www.frauenlauftreffrudow.de
Avon Running Berlin, see:
   www.frauen-lauf.de
Run, Lola, Run, dir. Tom Tykwer,
   Germany 1998

Running makes you happy and healthy, even if it won't make you rich.

Run-of-the-mill

oases

"Bankrupt architecture, a run-of-the-mill product, created not by architects but engineers," complained novelist Brigitte Reimann about the satellite towns that sprung up out of nowhere. Franziska Linkerhand, architect and novel heroine, is slowly losing her youthful verve as she works on dilapidated construction sites. She is an early—albeit fictional—representative of the rare species of female architects. The face of our cities is almost always determined by men. But women in the profession often find a good middle ground between the cult of genius of the major architects and the lack of imagination of the strictly functional buildings. Even though no one denies these days that the run-of-the-mill housing built in the prefab concrete high-rise style was justified at the time to ease the housing shortage (➤ **Prefab high-rise**), there are many examples of alternatives that worked.

As part of the International Building Exhibition in the 1980s, Inken Baller and her husband built public housing with beautiful filigree work along the canal in Kreuzberg. She stresses that women architects are more problem-oriented, giving more consideration to needs of the future residents than their more façade-oriented male colleagues.

The result is residential housing that unfolds its aesthetic meaning by focusing on the tenants. For example, the Kreuzberg apartments built by the internationally renowned architect Zaha Hadid, the first and—to date—only woman to receive the highest honor for architects, the Pritzker Prize. Hadid has built spectacular buildings around the world. Or the dynamic Béguinage built on Erkelenzdamm by Barbara Brakenhoff. Demographic developments show a need for such forward-looking designs for cooperative styles of living in the city (➤ **Beguines**).

Location
Stresemannstrasse 105–109,
10117 Berlin

How to get there
S- and U-Bahn,
Bus 200 Potsdamer Platz

Sources
Cornelia Carstens, Margret Luikenga, and Stephanie von Ow, *Immer den Frauen nach!*, ed.

Berliner Geschichtswerkstatt e. V., Berlin 1993

Brigitte Reimann, *Franziska Linkerhand* (novel), Berlin: Verlag Neues Leben, 1974

To find out more

Sonia Ricon Baldessarini, *Wie Frauen bauen. Architektinnen von Julia Morgan bis Zaha Hadid*, Berlin: Aviva Verlag, 2001

www.fopa.de

Tomatoes

oases

With the legendary tomato tossed by Sigrid Damm-Rüger at the Congress of the Socialist German Student Association (SDS) in 1968 in Frankfurt, the second-wave German women's movement had entered the stage of the '68 generation. The male comrades were not amused. They wanted to liberate everyone and everything–themselves, sexuality, workers, farmers, the Third World. But they remained consistently conservative in their dismissal of women's demands for emancipation and fair treatment as trivial and ridiculous. Berlin's Action Council for Women's Liberation wanted to discuss the matter with the men, who considered the idea unreasonable. Power relations between the sexes were a blind spot in theory and practice.

The women went their own way–which led through daycare centers and women's centers, action councils and alternative groups, bookstores and magazines. They forged ahead with an insatiable hunger for reading, consciousness-raising, exchange, analysis, and patriarchy critique; for resistance, activism, and imaginative alternatives. The slogan of the day was: The personal is political. What women experienced within their own four walls, in their marriages and families, in their education and on the labor market, was recognized as a product of politics, tradition, and men's claim to power, and thus removed from the haze of what was natural and divinely ordained. Such an analysis was too much for the Marxist comrades. Their gender-political incompetence reached its pinnacle when they declared that "whoever sleeps with the same person twice is part of the Establishment." Oh well. Every decade the heroes emotionally commemorate their rebellious youth. Best of all was the nude photo of Commune 1 resident Uschi Obermaier on the cover of *Stern*. What more could women want?

Location
Residence of "Commune 1," Stuttgarter Platz at Kaiser-Friedrich-Strasse, 10627 Berlin

How to get there
S 5, 7, 9 Charlottenburg

To find out more

http://de.wikipedia.org/wiki/
Aktionsrat_zur_Befreiung_
der_Frau

Wie weit flog die Tomate? Eine 68erinnen-Gala der Reflexion, ed. Heinrich Böll Foundation and the Feminist Institute, Berlin 1999

Ute Kätzel, *Die 68erinnen. Porträt einer rebellischen Frauengeneration*, Berlin: Rowohlt Verlag, 2002

Where it all began! Sexual liberation at Stuttgarter Platz

Under the bamboo roof

oases

There are at least 11,000 people of Vietnamese descent officially living in Berlin, most of them in the Lichtenberg and Marzahn-Hellersdorf districts. Even today the Vietnamese community in Berlin is largely divided between East and West: former boat people from South Vietnam in the West; and former contract workers and their families, mostly from North Vietnam, who worked in East Berlin. The boat people and their families are generally well-integrated. They received residence and work permits upon arrival, as well as language classes and training programs. The contract workers, in contrast, were originally supposed to leave the country after five years. When the Berlin Wall came down, they received residence permits that were tied to other conditions. For example, they had to be able to finance themselves. Many earn a hard living with flower or grocery stores, market stands selling clothing, or snack bars.

Under the Bamboo Roof, a women's project in Alt-Hohenschönhausen, is an oasis of relief where former contract workers meet and support each other.

Vinaphunu is specifically for Vietnamese women. Here women can learn German, and a social worker is there to help them find a job or apartment, resolve pregnancy or marital problems, advise them in childrearing questions, and help in dealing with the authorities. The group also offers free legal counseling with an interpreter, a book and video lending library, group trips, and the annual Tet festival for the Vietnamese New Year.

Integration problems among Vietnamese are rarely discussed publicly. Since education plays an important role in their culture, the children are often among the best in their class in Berlin; many parents stay in a country still foreign to them for the sake of their children (➤ **Multiculti**).

Location
Unterm Bambusdach,
Frauenprojekt der Bürgerinitiative
Ausländische MitbürgerInnen e.V.,
Neustrelitzer Straße 63,
13055 Berlin

How to get there
Tram M 6 Genslerstrasse or
Arendsweg,
Bus 256 Liebenwalder Strasse

Sources
www.multikulti.de/dossier/
   sommer/ein_tag_vietnam.html
www.vinaphunu.de

To find out more
Uta Beth and Anja Tuckermann, *Heimat ist da, wo man verstanden wird. Junge VietnamesInnen in Deutschland*, Berlin: Archiv der Jugendkulturen e. V., 2008

Thuy Nonnemann et al., *Vietnamesen in Berlin. Exil und neue Heimat*, ed. Ausländerbeauftragte des Berliner Senats, Berlin 1997

Appendices

Name index

Anna Wilhelmine of Anhalt-Dessau 210
Arnim, Bettina von 170, 210
Artemisia II of Caria 198
Augusta of Saxe-Weimar-Eisenach,
    Queen of Prussia 30
Baller, Inken 222
Beese, Melli 22, 24
Behrens, Constanze 58
Bloch, Kläre 62
Brakenhoff, Barbara 222
Brecht, Bertolt ..... 58 f.
Breitling, Gisela 44
Breth, Andrea ..... 58 f.
Campanini, Barberina 210
Cauer, Minna 190
Courths-Mahler, Hedwig 78
Damm-Rüger, Sigrid 224
Danz, Tamara 26
Dehmel, Paula and Richard 98
Dietrich, Marlene 22, 58, 110, 120
Domröse, Angelica 58

Dorka, Gertrud 14, 24
Drosner, Verena 58
Ebner-Eschenbach, Marie von 24
Einstein, Albert 60
Elisabeth Christine of Brunswick,
    Queen of Prussia 28
Encke, Wilhelmine 210
Fassbinder, Rainer Werner 120
Fellenberg, Dirk 12
Feuerherm, Wanda 62
Foster, Jodie 120
Frank, Charlotte 36
Frankenthal, Käte 24, 82
Freud, Sigmund 92
Friederike Luise of Hesse-Darmstadt,
    Queen of Prussia 210
Friedrich II, King of Prussia 110, 210
Friedrich Wilhelm I,
    Elector of Brandenburg 202, 210
Friedrich Wilhelm II, King of Prussia 210
Friedrich Wilhelm III, King of Prussia 30

Friedrich Wilhelm IV, King of Prussia 170
Gabin, Jean 110
Gentileschi, Artemisia 198
Goethe, Johann Wolfgang von 116
Grönemeyer, Herbert 12
Haberlandt, Fritzi 58
Hadid, Zaha 222
Hagen, Nina 42
Hahn, Otto 60
Hahnemann, Helga 42
Heinroth, Katharina 24
Hendel, Annekatrin 120
Henkel, Karin 58
Herz, Henriette 32
Heuwer, Herta 12
Höch, Hannah 10, 128
Hoppe, Marianne 58
Hoss, Nina 58
Humboldt
- Adelheid von 116
- Alexander von 116

- Caroline von ... 116
- Constanze von ... 116
- Gabriele von ... 116
- Marie Elisabeth von ... 116
- Wilhelm von ... 116
Hunzinger, Ingeborg ... 88
Jacobs, Helene ... 62
Jacoby, Hildegard ... 62
Jünger, Ernst ... 78
Kaléko, Mascha ... 144
Kaminer, Olga ... 132
Kaminer, Wladimir ... 132
Kauffman, Angelica ... 116
Kidman, Nicole ... 120
Klein, Anne ... 66
Kohl, Helmut ... 36
Kollwitz, Käthe ... 128, 214
Konnopke, Max ... 12
Krepl, Josefine Edle von ... 211
Langhoff, Shermin ... 58
Laserstein, Lotte ... 128

Laue, Max von ... 60
Lauenberger, Erna ... 136
Leibniz, Gottfried Wilhelm ... 28
Lorez, Gudula ... 92
Luise Henriette of Orange ... 210
Luise of Mecklenburg-Strelitz,
    Queen of Prussia ... 30, 116
Lustig, Henriette ... 160
Luxemburg, Rosa ... 18, 178
Mammen, Jeanne ... 128
May, Karl ... 78
Meitner, Lise ... 60
Méritt, Laura ... 112
Merkel, Angela ... 36
Modersohn-Becker, Paula ... 128
Morgenstern, Lina ... 190
Nathan, Helene ... 24
Nick, Désirée ... 42
Nickel, Maria ... 62
Nikutta, Sigrid ... 162
Obermaier, Uschi ... 224

Oppenheimer, Julius ... 98
Planck, Max ... 60
Potente, Franka ... 120
Rauch, Christian Daniel ... 116
Reimann, Brigitte ... 222
Rieck, Ursel ... 172
Riemenschneider, Tilman ... 74
Rois, Sophie ... 58, 120
Salomon, Alice ... 154
Schadow, Friedrich Wilhelm von ... 116
Schaeder, Hildegard ... 62
Schell, Helene von ... 62
Schiller, Charlotte ... 116
Schiller, Friedrich ... 116
Schinkel, Karl Friedrich ... 116
Schneider, Romy ... 76
Schragenheim, Felice ... 40
Schröder, Gerhard ... 36
Schulte, Axel ... 36
Schüttler, Katharina ... 58
Schwarzer, Alice ... 76, 93

Schygulla, Hanna	120
Selbert, Elisabeth	50
Siewert, Clara	128
Sophie Charlotte of Hanover, Queen of Prussia	28
Staewen, Gertrud	62
Steinmetz, Melanie	62
Sürücü, Hatun	84, 182
Tuaillon, Louis	8
Tucholsky, Kurt	210
Twiggy	86
Tykwer, Tom	120, 221
Ury, Else	166 ff.
Varnhagen, Rahel	32
Voltaire	110
Wabnitz, Agnes	158
Waldoff, Claire	42, 184
Waltz, Sasha	58
Wedding, Alex	136
Weigel, Helene	58 f.
Weiskopf, Grete	136
Wiener, Sarah	202
Wilhelm I, German Kaiser	8, 20, 100, 158
Winkelmann, Emilie	200
Winkler, Angela	58
Wolf, Friedrich	76
Wolzogen, Caroline von	116
Wust, Lilly	40
Ziegler, Regina	120
Ziervogel, Waltraud	12

Subject index

Aimée & Jaguar	40	
Alex	136	
Almancilar	104	
Amazon	8	
Anne and her three husbands	74	
Artemisia	198	
Baby of the family	166	
Beguines	200	
Berlin air	138	
Berlin flower	42	
Big mouth, big heart	106	
Birthing center	108	
Book of the Poor	170	
Boulette and mocca faux	202	
Business by and for women	140	
Caterpillar, cobra, columbine	142	
Chocolate	204	
Clio	44	
Cyanide	76	
Dada	10	
Dime-novel dreams	78	
Diva	12	
Dogs	80	
Dream figure	172	
Ewa, Frieda, Paula, Marie …	46	
Excavating the past	14	
Expecting	174	
Facts of life	82	
Fisimatenten	110	
For rent	112	
Fortuna	16	
Freedom	18	
Furies	176	
Girls from the office	144	
Girls move	206	
Gold rush	146	
Golden girl	20	
Green Minna	178	
Green thumbs	114	
Gypsies	180	
Headscarves	48	
High above the clouds	22	
Honor	84	
Humboldt	116	
Hungering for knowledge	24	
Ideal	86	
Knut	88	
Lisa and Jackie	118	
Lola	120	
Maiden	122	
Mannequins	148	
Mothers	50	
Mount Rubble	26	
Multiculti	124	
Neighborhood moms	54	
No special treatment	150	
Not my bag	182	
Nuns	90	
Out in the boondocks	208	
Out, out, out …	184	
Outside	186	
Painting ladies	128	
Paradise	212	

Pietà	214
Prefab high-rise	216
Prima donna	218
Pleasure	92
Polionauts …	130
Public money	56
Queens	28
Queer	94
Red-light	188
Rose	96
Run, Lola, Run!	220
Run-of-the-mill	222
Russian disco	132
Salon	32
Second Life	34
Showtime	58
Soccer	152
Social work	154
Softly, Peterkin, softly …	98
Soup-kitchen Lina	190
Splitting the atom	60
The milkmaid's calculations	156
The Wall	192
Tomatoes	224
Treadling like crazy	158
Twinkle toes	100
U-boats	62
Under the bamboo roof	226
ÜPFI	64
Washerwomen	160
Washing machine	36
Witches' breakfast	66
Woman of the Year Award	68
Women at the helm	162
Women's quarter	70
Working girls	194

Montage photo credits

Pages 6/7
Rahel Varnhagen: from Wikimedia Commons, http://projects.exeter.ac.uk/gutzkow/Gutzneu/gesamtausgabe/Archiv/Bilder/ZeiGutz/VarnhR1g.jpg
Federal Chancellery: © Bernd Kröger – Fotolia.com
Rosa Luxemburg: from Wikimedia Commons
Rumpler Taube: Jürgen Krämer
Amazon: from de.wikipedia.org, *Meyers Konversations-Lexikon* of 1885–1890

Pages 38/39
Lise Meitner: Helmholtz-Zentrum Berlin
Kläre Bloch: Kläre-Bloch-Schule, Berlin

Pages 72/73
The Holy Kinship: www.heiligenlexikon.de
Tango: from Wikimedia Commons, Schorle, de.wikipedia.org/wiki/Datei:Cachafaz.jpg
Hedwig Courths-Mahler: German Historical Museum, Berlin
Käte Frankenthal: Bezirksamt Neukölln von Berlin, Heimatmuseum archives

Pages 102/103
Portrait: © 47media - Fotolia.com

Pages 134/135
Telephone: German Wikipedia/Bran
World Clock: © moonrun – Fotolia.com
Washerwoman: from Wikimedia Commons, Heinrich Zille
Fashion photo: Bundesarchiv, Bild 183-E0905-0034-001, Zentralbild, Hochneder
Radio Tower: © Imken – Fotolia.com

Pages 164/165
Else Ury: Ernest Klaus Heymann Collection, London

Women: from Wikimedia Commons (source: http://www.frauenmediaturm.de/dossier_augspurg.html). From left to right: Anita Augspurg, Marie Stritt, Lily von Gizycki, Minna Cauer, and Sophia Goudstikker, ca 1896
Claire Waldoff: from Wikimedia Commons (source: Bundesarchiv, Bild 183-R07878/CC-BY-SA 3.0)
Wall: © fuxart – Fotolia.com

Pages 196/197
Bettina von Arnim: © Bildagentur bpk
Artemisia Gentileschi: from Wikimedia Commons (source: Web Gallery of Art, http://www.wga.hu/frames-e.html?/html/g/gentiles/artemisi)

My pearls

My pearls

Credits

Pearls on the River Spree
Berlin: City of Women

Published by
Gabriele Kämper,
Gender Equality Office,
Senatsverwaltung für Arbeit,
Integration und Frauen Berlin

Landesarbeitsgemeinschaft der bezirklichen Frauen- und Gleichstellungsbeauftragten Berlins

Project designed and directed by
Dr. Gabriele Kämper

Editorial team
Sylvia Edler
Heike Gerstenberger
Brigitte Heinrich
Brigitte Kowas
Christine Rabe
Regina Schmidt

Assisted by
Marion Winter

Copyediting
Jana Fröbel
Brigitte Heinrich
Anja Meierkord

English translation
Allison Brown
Kate Sturge

Photos
Kerstin Grune, Berlin
Except for the following:
Andreas Strauß (p. 119)
Team (pp. 13, 17, 41, 59, 77, 107, 159, 191, 225)
www.heiligenlexikon.de (p. 75)
www.graphoto.com (p. 211)

Graphic design, cover image, and montages
Kerstin Bigalke, Berlin, www.studiographoto.com

Maps
Kartopolis, www.kartopolis.de

Published by edition ebersbach 2012
www.edition-ebersbach.de

Printed by
Offizin Andersen Nexö, Leipzig

Printed in Germany
ISBN 978-3-86915-045-1